INSIDE MARRIAGE

A UNIQUE PORTRAIT OF MARRIAGE IN THE 90S

LINDA SONNTAG

INSIDE MARRIAGE

A UNIQUE PORTRAIT OF MARRIAGE IN THE 90S

LINDA SONNTAG

MANDARIN

A Mandarin Paperback

INSIDE MARRIAGE

Commissioning Editor: Sian Facer
Editors: Jane McIntosh, Loulou Brown
Art Editor: Peta Waddington
Production Controller: Antonia McArdle
Jacket photography: Lewis Mulatero

The publishers would like to thank Richard Ogden Limited, 28-29 Burlington Arcade, London
W1V 0NX for kindly lending the wedding rings used for jacket photography.

First published in Great Britain in 1994
by Mandarin Paperbacks,
an imprint of Reed Consumer Books Limited,
Michelin House, 81 Fulham Road, London SW3 6RB
and Auckland, Melbourne, Singapore and Toronto

A CIP catalogue record for this title is available from the British Library.

ISBN 0 7493 1801 5

Typesetting by ROM-Data Corporation Limited, Falmouth, Cornwall
Printed by Cox & Wyman Limited, Great Britain

Dedication

This book is dedicated with grateful thanks to the 302 people who contributed such frank and fascinating information about their married lives.

Thanks

I should like to thank Cathy Frazer for her help in sending out the questionnaires, and Jane McIntosh and Loulou Brown for their encouragement and their thoughtful comments and suggestions. L.S.

A note about the contributors to this survey

This book is based on two questionnaires, one entitled "How children affect your relationship", and the other called, simply, "Inside marriage". Contributors got hold of the questionnaires by writing in response to two articles in *The Daily Express* and to other articles in local papers from Bristol to Newcastle, or in response to appeals on local radio stations from Sussex to Merseyside.

There were 302 contributors, and 90 per cent of them were female. Ages ranged from 20s to 80s and size of family from one to nine, though the average age was 40, married to a man of 42, and the average family had two children. On average, the contributors had married at age 23, having known their partner well for nine months, and had their first child at 25, though the youngest to give birth was 16 and the oldest 39. The majority of women were in full-time employment, though most had taken some time off to look after their babies.

CONTENTS

LIFE TOGETHER 51

PREGNANCY 99

CHILDBIRTH   125

PARENTHOOD   137

INFIDELITY 185

INTRODUCTION

Marriage holds the greatest potential for a relationship between a man and a woman, promising lifelong love and security and a springboard from which both partners can go out into the world. It promises, but unfortunately, it does not always deliver. Currently, Britain has the highest divorce rate in Europe, with one in three marriages ending in divorce, and the average marriage lasting nine years. This book, based on a detailed survey of over 300 marriages, aims to investigate how and why marriage is failing.

Some of the marriages described here are inspiring; however roughly two thirds are broadly unsatisfactory. Most divorces (75 per cent) are instigated by women, and this survey confirms that the majority of women are dissatisfied with significant aspects of marriage. Though men were invited to take part, only one contributor in ten is male; what we have here is marriage seen through mainly female eyes.

Nine out of ten of us tries marriage at least once in our lives. Romantic and sexual love is held by society to be the ultimate personal fulfilment, and the pressure to form a couple is reflected in everything from government policy to the images of advertising. Women feel this pressure more than men. Single women are not prized by society; depending on their financial standing and the force of their personality, they are seen as either a failure or a threat — there is no female equivalent of "eligible". Biology also plays its part, allowing women less time than men in which they can choose parenthood. For these reasons, marriage is still a woman's passport into the mainstream of life, and even a negative relationship can seem more acceptable than none.

Since the revolution in female contraception of the 1960s and 1970s with the advent of the Pill, choices have opened up to women other than being permanently tied to home and family. Three-quarters of women between college-leaving age and retirement age are in the workforce. Women's lives are expanding into what was traditionally the male domain. Women in careers and jobs are continuing to break down one of the most important barriers between the sexes. The major plea from women to men in this book is that men should join them in breaking down these barriers, and begin to explore the territory that tradition tells us is the female domain.

Women's expectations of marriage have increased significantly over the spell of one generation. In the 1950s women were looking for husbands who would provide them with a decent roof over their heads, in return for which they would keep a decent house. Today's woman is usually capable of financing her own roof; what she is looking for is a man who will be her partner in a shared rich emotional life.

And this is where the problem lies. Masculinity, as we know it, is not about sharing, and it is not about emotions. It's about a mental strength that depends on suppressing and denying the emotions in order to succeed. It's also about physical strength. In the beginning, men evolved these strengths out of necessity. In primitive times women would have spent all their brief adult lives bearing and caring for offspring; it was vital that they should stay close to the home, gathering roots and berries, while the man's part was to go further afield and hunt and kill to provide. Men had to be powerful and single-minded to survive. And power and single-mindedness are still the hallmarks of traditional masculinity.

The institution of marriage, as we know it today, took root in the Industrial Revolution in the latter part of the eighteenth century in the comfortable homes of a new middle class of wealthy managers. While the man went out to compete in the hard-nosed world of business, the woman stayed at home, ran the house and reared large numbers of children, helped by servants. Meanwhile, in the working classes, men and women toiled shoulder to shoulder for very little pay. Their domestic arrangements were much looser, as men could not afford to make permanent commitments, but had to go wherever there was work.

The size of his house and family and the comfort in which his wife presided were all-important indications of a wealthy man's status. During the nineteenth century it became increasingly important that nothing should threaten domestic respectability, which was protected by a rigid code of behaviour. Under this system, which today is known as "Victorian family values", women were ruthlessly exploited and "kept in their place". Men liked to believe that only they were capable of sexual pleasure, and if their wives and daughters were found to have infringed the moral code by committing adultery or bearing an illegitimate child, they would literally be thrown out on the street. The head of the house was supposed to procreate children, but otherwise he satisfied his sex drive with visits to brothels and to the women servants below stairs; pornography proliferated. The double standard was well and truly established.

In the twentieth century during the two world wars, women were needed in the workforce. In factories and offices and in the Forces they found a new equality. But the 1950s once more saw women putting on their aprons while men dominated the world of work. The advent of the Pill in the 1960s changed everything. Today women have broken out of the trap of continuous childbearing and are joint wage earners with their male partners. But while the role of women has been redefined, the role of men is far less well focussed.

Male aggression, which once ensured the survival of the family and the species, has ceased to be essential to domestic life. How men deal with their redundant aggression affects us all. Some men channel it creatively into their work, others release it in sport. Many do both. Men who have not learned to direct aggression usefully may express it in violence, either against society (nine out of ten crimes are committed by men), or in their own homes. The extent of child abuse and wife battering is only now becoming recognized. One survey says that 40 per cent of men use violence against their wives, another that one in ten women have been raped by their partners, and estimates of child abuse vary from between one victim in ten children to one in four.

Given these figures, there is surprisingly little evidence of domestic violence in this book. One battered wife (aged 67) sent back the questionnaire, explaining that she found it impossible to fill it in, and it may be that others felt like her and chose not to take part in the survey for the same reason.

Women are made to feel ashamed of being victims of violence, as if they had somehow "asked for it". Anyone seeing a 15 stone man beating up an 8 stone man would call the bigger man a bully, but if the 8 stone victim is his wife, then it's assumed to be somehow "her fault". And when it comes to domestic violence, the police are reluctant to intervene.

One reason that marital rape doesn't feature anywhere in this book may be that women who are raped by their husbands are conditioned by the male view, only recently overturned in the courts, that if sex is forced on you by your husband, it isn't rape. One woman writes that her partner forced her to have sex before she was ready after childbirth. She doesn't call it rape, but it is. There may be other similar unidentified cases.

At its least harmful, male aggression is no more than posturing machismo. "Macho" — perhaps best exemplified by Sean Connery playing James Bond — has always been a currency in all-male company, but as women have become increasingly independent, the "hard man" has lost much of his appeal for them.

Only two of the women who feature in this book appreciate macho qualities in men. The vast majority of contributors are looking for a new notion of masculinity, in which male strength depends, as female strength has always done, on self-knowledge – accepting instead of suppressing vulnerability and weakness. Overwhelmingly, women say that they like a man who can cry. They like a man who is in tune with his feelings and can talk about how he feels. They like a man who involves himself with family life and who is as committed as they are to children and home.

But the "New Man" – the man who pushes his little daughter in her buggy as fast as he can because it makes her squeal with laughter, and never mind the stares, and who thinks nothing of going into a crowded shop to ask for a packet of Tampax – is pretty thin on the ground. Although men are beginning to recognize that it's unreasonable to expect a woman in full-time employment also to be totally responsible for the housework, cooking and childcare while they relax after a busy day, they are doing very little about taking some of the necessary chores away from their partners and doing the work themselves. Men spend less than half as much time on housework as their female partners, and their involvement in childcare is still minimal. One recent survey found that only one per cent of couples divide cooking, food-shopping and laundry equally. Even in a household where there is a degree of sharing, it won't be the man who takes the day off to look after the sick child, or to wait at home for the washing machine to be repaired.

Far from taking joint responsibility for the running of home and family, most men seem to add to their partners' workload. Women describe themselves as constantly clearing up after men who leave behind them full ashtrays and dirty cups and glasses, floors strewn with wet towels and dirty clothes. There are exceptions, of course, but a picture gradually emerges in this book of the typical 1990s husband as a slob. In one of the most interesting questions, contributors were asked to say what they liked least about their partners. The answers from women pointed overwhelmingly to slobbish behaviour: here we see men sprawling in front of the television among dirty crockery, picking their noses, their ears, their nails, and flicking the dirt, and deliberately farting and belching. Some women were timid about these revelations – would they be thought ridiculous to complain? Was this sort of behaviour too trivial to mention? Was it perhaps even funny?

It's not funny or trivial, because it's done deliberately to disgust. It's aggressive behaviour, masquerading as "natural" and hence unobjectionable behaviour, and it seems so widespread as to be part of the male armory of abuse. If this behaviour were natural, it would be common to both sexes, which it isn't. So why do men indulge in such deliberately objectionable personal behaviour? The answer is because *it's a way of exercising power*. To intrude on your partner's sensibilities is a way of offending against her femininity, a way of dominating her that she feels almost impossible to complain about, because she feels it's her fault for being sensitive. A man who behaves like this literally makes himself bigger, by creating a zone around himself that's full of repulsive sights, sounds and smells. He forces the sensitive person – his partner – to recognize his power by making her skirt round him. Later, she is humiliated into clearing up his mess. He has put her well and truly "in her place".

This example of machismo is symptomatic of how some men in this apparent age of equality feel the need privately to undermine women, in order to prove themselves still "head of the household".

Many of the men described in this book exercise their power in another way against their partners: through silence and withdrawal. Men who refuse to participate in the running of home and family, or refuse to share their thoughts and feelings, tend to clam up when their partners want to talk about these issues. The typical course of an argument runs like this: woman identifies topic for discussion; man denies its validity; woman insists; man accuses his partner of "nagging"; woman becomes angry and upset; man walks away. The effect of stonewalling is to make a woman desperate to be heard. If what she is saying is not considered worth hearing, she is made to feel unworthy of consideration herself. The woman is belittled, and again the man has made himself feel "big", too big to be bothered with her concerns.

A very damaging male withdrawal often takes place after the birth of a baby. Again there are moving exceptions, but it is quite common for a new father to refuse to be involved with his baby and to act like a jealous elder brother who has been pushed out of number one place by its arrival. The new father who is not prepared for the responsibilities of parenthood often reverts to a bachelor existence in protest, coming home after work only to eat, then spending night after night out with his mates, drinking or playing squash. These two activities cropped up repeatedly in this context. It could be that the jealous father has a subconscious desire to outdrink the infant suckling at the breast he used to consider "his" (men are often described as being jealous of breastfeeding); and the sudden passionate interest in the violent game of *squash* (one man played seven nights a week after his baby was born) would seem to speak for itself.

A significant proportion of the mothers who contributed to this book were turned into virtual single parents by their husbands' lack of support. Some women describe their partners as being like extra children to look after; one husband and father of four describes himself as "the lodger". On top of this extra burden of work and responsibility, mothers who stay at home to look after their children, even for a couple of years, worry that they are devaluing their earning power and will not be able to return to work at the same level. And were their partners to leave, they would no longer be able to earn enough to support themselves and their children.

The disintegration of the family – one family in five is cared for by a single parent, and nine out of ten single parents are women – has become a topic of hot public debate. The government's contribution is to launch a campaign called "Back to basics", which advocates a return to the "family values" of the 1950s. But the 1950s, the era of so-called decency, was the era in which women stayed home chained to the sink. In times of recession, such as we are now experiencing in the early 1990s, a moral crusade often rears its head, simply because there is not enough cake in the national economy to go round. Predictably, a right-wing government made up almost entirely of men is advocating that women should regress 40 years and chain themselves once again to the sink – that way, there'll be more cake to feed the men (especially those men who already have the lion's share). But going backwards would not be a useful move, even if this were possible. Instead of women going backwards, men should move forwards.

There is abundant evidence in this book to show that marriage is in crisis because women are not adequately supported by men in running the home and family – indeed men are often seen to be actively undermining their partners. It should come as no surprise to readers to learn that married women die earlier than single women, while married men live longer than single men.

In this book there are some women who show how marriage can be made to work, but the majority record exactly why and how their love and respect for men dwindle and die. Their accounts explain why it is that women instigate more than three-quarters of all divorces, despite the overwhelming personal, social and economic hardship of becoming single mothers.

The women in this survey are inviting men to question what masculinity means, and to redefine it within their relationships in terms of participation instead of power, involvement instead of aggression, responsibility instead of withdrawal. Women want men to find strength in their weaknesses and to learn to share a fuller emotional life.

How will men respond to this invitation? However rich the rewards of intimacy, will they be enough to compensate for loss of status in the eyes of the traditional male world, and for the work involved in sharing care of home and family, and for the self-doubt that is part of the process of opening up into self-knowledge? It is a difficult challenge that women are asking men to accept, but if they refuse it, what is the future for marriage?

LOVE

Love is life's prize; romantic and sexual love is held by the society in which we live to be the ultimate personal fulfilment. Today, everything is geared towards coupledom, from government policy to adverts for cars. But true love is elusive and rarely eternal – divorce statistics show us that. What do we mean by love? Can it last? Are our expectations of it perhaps too high?

Q: Was it love at first sight?

Around one in four say it was. In a few remarkable cases the conviction was so strong that it was "commitment at first sight".

"Yes, definitely. The first time I saw him I told everyone – that is the man I am going to marry."

The strength of one man's convictions still puzzles his widow:

"I think it must have been for him, because he proposed after our first date, and we didn't even hold hands! Proposed again next day over the phone. We got engaged after six weeks. I didn't understand how it was that he knew for certain that we were meant for each other and it is still a mystery to me."

It seems incredible that people can make an instant prediction that they will share a lifetime with a total stranger, and be proved right. Another woman writes:

"Yes, our first night out together, I knew this was the man I was going to marry. I had a feeling of total trust in him. I think true love deepens with knowledge, but I was in love that first night."

Trust implies familiarity. One of the most potent aspects of being in love is the almost surreal combination of being reassured by the familiar and at the same time fascinated by the unfamiliar. It excites and heightens all the senses. They become highly receptive to inflexions of voice, small gestures, looks, hesitations, posture. Every nuance of a person's body language and appearance feeds information not only about his or her economic, social and educational background, but more importantly about their emotional history. It is this coded information that "clicks", as so many people put it, with their own biographical data.

We often make friends in the same way, becoming instantly drawn to people, and then finding to our surprise that we have many experiences in common.

But falling in love can be cataclysmic, especially if you happen to be married to someone else already:

"Yes. I walked into the pub where he was working (I was with my previous husband of three years at the time, in a marriage that I thought was OK) and I knew immediately that this was it. I fell in love right there and then."

"Yes, but as both of us were in faithful partnerships at the time, the feeling was not allowed freedom."

"No, not with my husband. But seven years ago I met a man, face to face, and believe I genuinely fell in love with him. My feelings are a mixture of great joy and deep pain."

Strong and lasting bonds can be forged at a very early age:

"Almost, on my part – I was eleven years old, but he hardly deigned to notice me then!"

The dominant, and for many people the first, ingredient in falling in love is sexual attraction. The biological advantage in choosing a partner you "click with", is that it maximizes the chances of staying together to look after any children.

"Attraction at first sight would be more appropriate."

"Almost – certainly very attracted to him; I don't know whether that is love at first sight."

"Flirtation and lust, but I don't think love."

"No, but I was attracted to his fun personality on first meeting."

"Yes, the chemistry between us hit straight away."

"Yes, I fancied him something rotten."

However, though none actually disliked their partners at the beginning, the majority did not recognize instantly how close they would become. Instead, the awareness built up gradually, then suddenly surfaced, taking them by surprise.

"No. We met on a completely blind date and we both agree we thought each other 'alright'. No great physical attraction on either side. His main memory of our first meeting was that I was the shortest girl he'd ever been out with!"

"No, it was about six weeks before we felt good together. We both had doubts during the first weeks."

"No. I was fascinated, though, by this man whose wife I knew had just committed suicide."

"No. I worked with my husband for two years before we got together, and I just looked on him as a colleague – probably because he was already married to someone else."

"Definitely not. My partner grew on me, as my love for him has."

One woman provides a very different and intriguing answer:

"No. Fell in love over the telephone."

And one man replies that he and his wife fell in love while writing letters to one another during the Second World War. Falling in love with someone you can't see is unusual, but is by no means as unlikely as it sounds.

Talking to people face to face is a complex activity, fraught with anticipating and reacting to their body language. Shyness or a desire to be liked tend to tailor the message and its delivery according to the listener. But when talking on the telephone and writing letters, we have no visual feedback. We are linking directly with the other person's mind. The phone and the written word are very intimate mediums of communication. Though some find this unnerving, it enables others to concentrate more fully on what they want to get across and express themselves with greater confidence.

This woman doubts whether her feelings really "qualify" as love:

"No, but an instant rapport developed from talking to each other. It was a

3

gut feeling that he was/is someone I instantly felt at ease with. When we married I wasn't even sure I loved him, as if I'm honest, I don't think I know what love really is. I'd say that if this empty and not totally happy feeling I have when my husband and I are apart is love, then I love him."

She is one of several people who say they don't know what love is. Being in love is a risky business, and some people have learned to safeguard themselves against powerful emotions that they fear could overwhelm them and sweep them away.

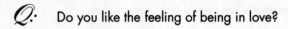

Q: Do you like the feeling of being in love?

Predictably, most people enjoy being in love, assuming, of course, that the feeling is reciprocated. A widow of 80 begins a series of typical replies:

"It is the ultimate ecstasy."

"There is no feeling like it – you feel you can conquer the world, and everything looks rosy. You feel radiant, sexy, confident – and you look it too."

"Yes, it gives you a glowing feeling and makes you more tolerant of other people."

"Yes, it's a lovely feeling, warm and secure."

"Very much. At first it was quite explosive. Now it's a very secure warm feeling."

"Yes, it makes you feel young and able to tackle anything."

"Yes, it made me lose weight."

"Yes, it makes me feel worthwhile as a person."

The main reason people give for enjoying being in love is a feeling of being at the centre of things. This pleasurable sense of your own strength makes you take a generous view of the failings of others: you ride smoothly over life's irritations.

But other people talk of the addictive, blindly out-of-control element of being in love. Powerful sex hormones take over and can dangerously distort the perceptions:

"Yes, it's exciting and worrying at the same time."

"Yes, but sometimes it feels so good that I'm afraid the bubble might burst! He's away at sea five months, at home three months. Absence makes the heart grow fonder."

"Yes, although the intensity can sometimes be overwhelming."

"Not sure. It's crazy."

"In some ways, but not too happy that it is an overpowering emotion which, for a time, makes one neglect other aspects of life."

"No, not now. When I was a teenager it was fun, but age and some bad experiences have taught me not to allow my heart to rule my head."

"No – I hate having no control over my emotions and reactions. Of course I felt quite differently at 16 – I revelled in it."

"From what I remember, yes, although I didn't like the feeling that I would perish if I didn't spend the rest of my life with him."

Two contributors have guarded against the dangers of overpowering love and never allowed themselves to feel acutely:

"I like the feeling of being wanted, needed and respected. What is 'love' exactly?"

"I have never been totally in love. I have been in relationships where I have felt committed and loved someone a lot, but not 'in love' with them."

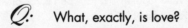

Q: What, exactly, is love?

As we saw in the last question, being in love is a dynamic condition that veers between a feeling of almost superhuman power at one end of the scale, and extreme vulnerability at the other. At one moment you are at the centre of the universe, beaming out rays of heat to its darkest corners; at the next you are dashed on the rocks in a cold, barren place. Your well-being is totally dependent on the whims of another: a smile can bathe you in glory, while a doubting look or a neglectful silence will have you hurtling into outer space.

It's a drastic condition, unsettling to the core of your being, which is why some people who enjoy being in control of their lives and have experienced it already, don't relish the prospect of falling in love again. In fact, being in love is in very many ways like returning to babyhood. When things are going well, the baby really is at the centre of his universe, warm, suckling at the breast, surrounded by love. But if he is hungry and his mother is out of sight, he is plunged into desperation and misery, and cries as if his life depends on her return – which, in a very real way, it does. In falling in love, we seem to have regained the original paradise of a very close, exclusive and blissfully nourishing union with another person – but with it, inevitably, comes the fear that if that person subsequently rejects us, we will perish.

Although the feelings are acutely real, the visions of heaven and hell conjured up by being in love are an illusion, which is why the illogical behaviour of lovers can seem laughable or even insane to their friends. The truth is that most adults can and do survive rejection, and if the relationship becomes established, and the irrational fear of death has passed, the positive side of being in love also has a chance to emerge from its intoxicated swoon-like stage and enter into a new phase of consciousness.

Sometimes you can wake up from the colourful perfumed haze of being in love and wonder what on earth you saw in the person you were previously infatuated with. At other times the emotions might develop into a deeper form of love.

The contributors to this survey had very similar views on what, exactly, love is. Here are some of them:

"Wow! Enjoying each other's company, sharing yourself, caring, empathizing and being prepared to listen and take part in the other person's sorrows and joys. Laughing together."

"Sharing moments that might be embarrassing with anyone else."

"Wanting to share everything of yourself, everything that happens to you, everything you are, ever have been and will be with someone who makes your world glow with light, happiness and contentment."

"Caring is indirectly a form of self-sacrifice. Love is trusting someone implicitly and attempting to understand their needs over and above your own."

"Being with someone who feels like your twin spirit, mentally, emotionally and physically."

"Even after 14 years together as a married couple, looking forward to hearing the key in the door – the unexpected phonecall."

"Feeling extremely alive, invigorated, healthy, happy, attractive, confident that he is feeling the same as you do."

"Thinking about someone 24 hours a day. Wild passion. Thinking you're the only two people in the world, and that you would die if he died. Total acceptance – loving even his faults. Squeezing his zits with care and tenderness!"

"Feeling warm, comfortable in [his] company, an inner glow, knowing that even without make-up, your hair in rats and a red nose, he still thinks you're stunning!"

Finally, here's a thoughtful answer from a young mother:

"Love is very difficult to define, like most feelings, I suppose. Completing this questionnaire has been good as it makes me realize how lucky I am in my marriage. At times things seem hard, what with coping with nine-month-old twins in a small flat, no work, no money, no prospects of moving etc., and the pressure has made us argue more, but I never really worry about the arguments because I know how deep and strong our love is. I count myself very lucky to have found a man like my husband, as from what I see there are not many decent men out there. It depresses me to see how many people have affairs etc. I cannot understand how they put everything at risk, just for momentary excitement. I know mistakes are made and people are only human, but it still depresses me. Also, I feel a stable relationship is so important when it comes to having and bringing up children. A lot of people seem to take having children so lightly, and inevitably it's the children that suffer through break-ups and bad feeling."

These were some of the more individual contributions. Many degenerated into cliché (one woman even spoke of fluffy toys and heart-shaped pillows), which seems to indicate how much "love" is a received idea, something we all feel we must subscribe to in order to be both socially acceptable and also acceptable to ourselves.

Q: Are you still in love with your partner?

A lot of people answered "yes" here, but their answers were not borne out by the rest of what they said in the questionnaire. People very much want to be still in love. To be *still* in love is seen as a personal "success" in a society that offers people congratulations at each wedding anniversary. Is "love" really no more than an endurance test?

One woman says she feels no less in love today than she felt on her wedding day 48 years ago – but the rest of her answers are full of unhappiness with her neglectful husband. It is depressing to face the fact that you are staying in a loveless marriage.

Most of those who still love their partners say that the initial feeling of "in love" has mellowed over the years into something more serene.

"When you start a relationship, everything is interesting and exciting, because you are discovering a person you don't know everything about. Once you have been together for some time, common sense dictates that things will become less exciting, more tranquil and happy."

"No. You become comfortable. You don't need to swoon and look starry-eyed all the time."

"In the early days it was excitement, like a rush of adrenalin. This was eventually replaced by a feeling of tranquillity and happiness."

"Being on cloud nine at the beginning changes to love, respect and loyalty as the years advance."

This mature love can last a lifetime, and even endure beyond the grave.

"Mellowing love lasted through our lives together."

"Although it's coming up [for] seven years since she died, I still love her."

"My love for my husband endured over the whole of our 33 years together, and still does beyond the grave."

A handful of answers suggest that love has intensified rather than mellowed, strengthened rather than become – as for many – more "comfortable". These people have not so much "settled down", as continued to feel actively emotionally engaged with each other.

"Very much still in love (both of us are). This has deepened over the years and not diminished at all."

"Yes – it has changed over the years, but for the better. Romance and initial passion make way for a deeper, stronger love. The babies put pressure on our relationship, but that's nothing serious."

"Yes, but not the passionate love from the first few years. It's a far deeper feeling now."

For the remainder, love had dwindled or disappeared. Some put up with a loveless relationship, others left. Reading contributors' answers as a whole, it is probably fair to say that as many as two-thirds of the relationships described were largely unsatisfactory. Being taken for granted, feeling neglected and unsupported, feeling jealous – whether of another adult or of your partner's attention to your own children – are some of the reasons men and women fall out of love with each other. This book aims to investigate how and why – after powerful initial attraction – love flourishes or dies.

YOUR PARTNER

Although some still feel a negative relationship is better than no relationship at all, women's expectations of marriage have increased dramatically over the space of one generation. Today they are looking for partners with whom to share rich emotional lives – and they are coming up against a problem, because historically, men have been trained to suppress vulnerability to feelings, considering it a weakness. The women in this chapter are inviting men to talk, to listen, to share, to open up to sensuality and sexuality, and to explore the whole world of feeling that "macho" denies.

 What made you decide that this was the person you wanted to set up home with?

A small number of contributors married their childhood sweethearts, but most had a few other intimate relationships before they met their partners.

One or two made up their minds the moment they set eyes on each other that this was their match, and several more took only a few days or weeks to decide, but on average, it took nine months—interestingly—from first meeting to commitment.

For many, it was the discovery of a new quality of intimacy that made them realize that this was the person they wanted to set up home with. People know when they find the right person, because they seem to drop into place in a different dimension, a dimension in which they are totally accepted. It's a feeling of stillness and rightness where everything fits and makes sense, the eye of the storm of being in love.

"It just felt right together. I'd never felt like that before. Couldn't imagine not sharing my life with him."

"I felt totally at ease with him. No pretending, no trying to be what you're not. We fit together perfectly."

"Because this was a different feeling to all the others I had known – much more of an acceptance."

11

"Totally different to anyone else, more caring and loving, accepted me as a person."

"We both knew that this was it. We were so suited to each other and such good friends."

"I just felt totally comfortable with him and he seemed to have the same ideas and goals as me."

It's a feeling of permanence, almost of destiny, of taking your place in the scheme of things:

"All the feelings that ran through my mind and my body when I first saw him are still there. I knew I wanted to be with him forever and keep him close to me. I also knew immediately that I wanted children by him."

One man felt this sense of destiny as though it came from outside himself, rather than from within him and his partner:

"Foretold by writing in the sand, Tarot cards and palmistry. I was even given the initials of my wife's maiden name."

For others, less happily, it was not so much a sense of having met the right person, as of grasping an opportunity to make a welcome change in their lives.

"Being very unhappy at home, it was my way out."

"I was 32 and wanted children. He was very good looking, also reliable and honest."

"He gave me a sense of security. I liked his humour. He was there at exactly the right time."

"I wanted to get away from the parental home and was so flattered someone wanted me."

It seems that the feeling of being on the shelf can strike even the very young. One woman of 26 and another of 24 felt they were getting so old, they would not get another chance.

"I was getting on in years. I thought any man better than none."

"In fact when we decided to marry there was no romance – we discussed it like doing the shopping. Due to my lack of experience I thought that at 24 years old, if I didn't marry him, I would be left on the shelf and be alone for ever. Even on the eve of the wedding I panicked – I wanted to run away, but I felt that so much planning had been put into it that I would let too many people down and I told myself it would be alright – how wrong I was."

During the Second World War, many must have married to give themselves some hope to cling to, as did this woman, now 77, who had just been jilted after a four-year courtship:

"A need to be in love again and cared for, and fear of the future during the War."

Some got married for no very specific personal reasons at all: it was simply what their families and everybody else expected them to do.

"I don't think I ever did decide he was the right person. It was just expected we would marry. A sort of arranged marriage."

"I had known him since childhood. My parents spent their honeymoon in his parents' hotel. I knew he was sincere, honest, loyal, kind and, at that time, interesting. He was of good education and background."

One woman's head was turned by the promise of glamour and excitement:

"My ex was so different and he introduced me to many new experiences. I was in a whirl. I had lived a sheltered life and he made me feel grown-up (I was 21). These were the wrong reasons."

Another woman's head was screwed very tightly on to her shoulders. She was 23 and admits that neither she nor her partner were sexually attracted to one another when she made this calculating decision:

"My heart does not rule my head and I knew I would have to have money and security to make a lasting marriage. My husband put his studies before me and that decided me from our first date."

Some of those who got married despite the fact that they didn't "click" with their partner, realized at the time that they were missing out on the sense of rightness and deep mutual acceptance that forms the foundation of a lasting relationship. But they still did it. Why?

First, there is the pressure to conform. In a society where marriage is the norm, single people are outsiders. This is especially true of women. The adjective "eligible" is applied exclusively to bachelors; a woman on her own is regarded either as a failure or as a threat, depending on her economic status and the force of her personality. Marriage is the passport to acceptance into the mainstream of life.

Secondly, there is the deep human need to love and be loved, to form a circle of nurture and protection with another human being. For women, the time runs out in which they can pass on their love to the next generation. All relationships are imperfect, but for many, even a negative relationship is better than the feared prospect of loneliness.

 ### What were you looking for in a long-term partner?

A survey conducted in the 1950s concluded that the most important factors in choice were financial security and respectability. People wanted decent living standards and decent partners. A 58-year-old woman who married in the '50s confirms the findings of that survey. She writes that she was looking for:

"Someone who liked a nice home and knew his way around. Someone with a good job and prospects."

This sounds extremely old-fashioned in our age of equality. It shows how women have changed. Marriage is no longer about the woman keeping the house nice while her partner is out making his way in the world; it is about equality and sharing. Compatibility and personal fulfilment are what people are looking for from marriage today. They are hoping to enjoy themselves together.

Several contributors say that they were not looking for a partner at all: "Something clicked, and everything fell into place." But most were hoping to find lasting love and understanding.

"Deep love, close friendship, compatibility, shared interests. Fun!"

"Someone who really loved me and wanted to care for me. The feeling that we could make the marriage last through every problem, no matter what happened."

"Someone kind, gentle, caring, honest and truthful. Someone to look after."

"Someone whom you could trust and who would share a deep understanding of your own needs. Deep commitment and communication."

"Soulmate, helpmate, lover, friend."

"Togetherness, a sense of sharing. Security. Someone who could make me feel special."

"An equal."

"Someone who would not clip my wings. Who would respect my ideas/ career/thoughts equally, as I would theirs. Someone I would feel comfortable/ safe with, and – of utmost importance – someone I would trust implicitly."

"Genuine commitment to keep a good relationship alive. Humour and sensitivity. Good sex, and a demonstrative, loving father for our children."

It is partly because women want to share rich emotional lives with their partners, with good communication at all levels, that the divorce rate is much higher today than it was in the 1950s. Most divorces are instigated by women, indicating that it's the men who don't live up to these new standards.

Historically, men have been brought up to do exactly what women back in the 1950s still wanted them to do: provide, and be "head of the household". In order to be efficient and even ruthless providers, men have had to deny their vulnerability and suppress their emotions. Now women are inviting men to liberate those parts of their personalities that they have never previously expressed. It is perhaps not surprising that the majority find it difficult to open up.

The parents of the 1990s can do much for the next generation by helping their sons develop the emotional skills that they will need as adults.

 What similarities can you see between your partner and your opposite sex parent?

This was not a popular question, probably because people don't like the implication that they might have "married" their parents. However, some contributors did acknowledge similarities, both good and bad.

"Many similarities. Steadfastness, loyalty, faithfulness, complete trust, sense of humour, punctuality, honesty."

"Loads – stubborn, reliable, good with figures, finds it hard to apologize, faithful, works too hard, too hard on the children, can be fun when tries."

"Quite a lot! Intolerance towards the television, lack of acceptance that different people like different things. Quick temper. Good sense of humour. Trustworthy, honest, fair."

"Both very caring people and both strong emotionally."

"Moodiness."

"Stubborn. Says very little, doesn't share feelings. I'm supposed to guess his thoughts."

"The same birthday! My father was the only person in the world who had ever loved me, and this man seemed similar."

"Slight physical resemblance, kindness, gentleness, good manners."

"I didn't know my father, who died when I was three, but I think it's significant that he too was 20 years older than my mother."

The way our parents behave to us and to each other – their characteristics, attitudes, habits and moods – gives us our first emotional map, and when we meet its landmarks again in adult life, we recognize them as "home". These are the qualities we are familiar with, and to which we have some experience of relating.

We have already seen that familiarity is an important factor in choosing a partner (see page 1). It follows that a woman whose father was kind and affectionate will hold that image in her mind, and be drawn to kindness and affection when she finds it in another man.

But equally, a woman whose father was remote and unaffectionate, will tend to be drawn to a man who is like him. This is less easy to accept. There are, however, men who are cold and unemotional, and there are women who marry them, and wish they were more loving. Why do they make that choice in the first place?

It is useful, if you are always attracted to men who do not return your love, to understand that the reason may lie not, as you probably suspect, in your own bad judgment of character, but in your emotional conditioning from birth. If you tried and tried as a child to get your undemonstrative father to show that he loved you, it may be that your subconscious desire to resolve the original problem has led you to choose a man who is as unresponsive as your father was. Are you still trying to get through to the man in your life without success? Do you blame yourself for his coldness, because you think you're not trying hard enough? Do you blame yourself for always choosing the wrong type of man? (Similarly, a man might be attracted to a woman who is either overbearing or neglectful because that's what he was used to in his mother.)

A look at your family background may help explain some of the dynamics of your own relationship that puzzle and worry you. Understanding the root of your problem won't make it go away, though it will give you a new perspective and spare you from continuing to blame yourself.

The dominant influence may not come from the opposite sex parent. An interesting answer comes from a woman whose mother died when she was a baby. The qualities she sought in a partner were the "feminine" ones that she had missed as a child.

"Very few similarities. My dad is big, loud and very masculine. My husband is gentle and kind."

Other contributors recognized that they had been equally influenced by parental characteristics, but made a conscious effort to choose someone who would provide them with a totally different environment to the one in which they had grown up. These women chose men as unlike their fathers as possible.

"Not too many, I hope. Part of the attraction was that he was not too much like my father. We had a difficult relationship as we are a lot alike and that caused problems when I was growing up. He tried to be domineering and I would question that a lot. I was looking for a partner as little like that as possible. Someone who would be with me, not against me."

"None. I married my husband because he was the total opposite of my father and I didn't have much respect for my father as he was a rather weak character."

"Very few, thankfully. My father abused me."

"None at all, thankfully. My father is mean, boring and inconsiderate."

17

What similarities can you see between your relationship and that of your parents?

This question was felt to be less threatening than the one above, and elicited more replies. People did see similarities, good and bad, between their own relationship and the one in which they had grown up.

"It is quite similar: warm, loving, peaceful and a lot of fun and humour around the house. No violence at all."

"Loyalty – the first big romance of our lives."

"Inability to communicate."

"We now argue a lot, like my parents."

"Quite a few! HELP!! My mother is volatile, emotional, enjoys a laugh, fun etc. I can see [the possibility of] myself getting bored like my mother has from time to time with my step-dad."

"We have fallen into a rut and take each other for granted. We don't socialize much and lead a quiet life."

"Practical, too comfortable, too detached, lack of open passion, lack of compassion, too independent people."

"We don't talk or discuss close family problems."

"Sometimes fiery. Quick to make up generally. Lots of laughs. Both men fairly selfish."

Interestingly, some answers revealed how women's expectations of marriage have increased in the spell of one generation (see also page 14).

"We have a more equal relationship. My mother was dominated by my father, though this did even out a bit in later years. We have always had a very equal relationship. We come to joint decisions about major things, talking them through and coming to a compromise if necessary."

"Not so many, as my mother was of a much more passive generation. However, the passion I know they shared and the solicitous care my father took of her are similar."

"Love and commitment in both, but my parents' expectations of marriage were less than ours."

"Not too many. I talk a lot more than mum and put up with less! We both have a sense of duty, but mum's has seemed to prevent her from ever achieving her potential. I find my own goals important too."

And, as in the last question, others had made a conscious effort to choose a marriage that was the exact opposite of the original one in which they had spent their childhood.

"None. A conscious effort has been made not to follow the same pattern. My father was a womanizer and my parents divorced after 25 years of marriage. We are determined not to follow suit."

"My mum and dad split up when I was 11 and my mum remarried when I was 13. She was very much the weaker partner in both relationships, and it made me stronger in that I was determined to be on an equal footing with my partner. One of the main attractions of my husband has always been the total trust I have in him. I have a very strong sense of family, more so now that we have our own daughter. Because my parents' marriage failed, it made me realize that they can go wrong, and it makes me more determined that mine won't."

 Is marriage important, as opposed to living together? If so, why?

Most of the people who took part in this questionnaire were married, and took a conservative view on this subject. Despite the fact that two in three marriages do not last, only one contributor had a cynical view of marriage:

"No. Marriage is outdated, a subtle device of men to trap women into becoming their personal slaves."

And one other suggested an alternative:

"I think a lifetime with one man is too long. There should be a chance to review the contract every so often, both partners being made to air their views with a third party (with the least possible upset)."

Some make the point that personal commitment is more important than the paper certificate:

"I used to think it was, but I feel it's the quality of the commitment made rather than the title that goes with it."

"It isn't the certificate that counts, it's the commitment. You don't need a piece of paper to be committed to each other."

Others point out the practical convenience of marriage: it's a bond recognized in society and under law.

"It doesn't add to or detract from the relationship, which depends on the protagonists for its survival, but it does make life *easier* – joint names, introducing your husband, gives validity in the eyes of others."

"The only difference is in the law, and marriage makes you more secure financially."

And several say it's important if you are going to have children:

"It's only important if you want children."

"I think marriage is very important if there are children, otherwise not. It gives children a secure framework in which to develop their potential."

"Our relationship deepened further through marriage. It's important, I believe, for the children's sake. I would not have been happy having children outside marriage, though I don't knock people who do."

But the vast majority believe in the commitment of marriage per se. For some, it's a matter of religion; for others, it's an insurance against things going wrong, or at least, a reassurance that both parties will work hard to get them going right again.

"Private and public statement of commitment."

"To us it is very important. We place great emphasis on commitment. We want the stability and permanence of marriage. Without the vows, it could have been all too easy to walk away from the problems we have overcome. Marriage means you try harder to save a relationship. It's something worth fighting for."

"I know people say it's only a piece of paper, but to me marriage is a commitment. We have chosen each other for ever and have said so in front of witnesses and in front of God."

"I feel marriage is right for me. I see nothing wrong in living together, but feel that the commitment to a relationship for some people is stronger in marriage. It certainly is for me."

"Security. You feel you can't just walk out after a row. It also gives security to the children."

"I totally believe in the institution of marriage, because I feel you work a lot harder at keeping things together – that's why the other female is still on the outside."

A woman of 77 hits the nail on the head when she describes the psychological importance of the marriage vows:

"Yes, because it promises love, security, stability, social standing, social acceptance, protection for children – but it doesn't always fulfil its promises, as I was to find out."

 How much do you actually like your partner as a person? Would you say he or she was your best friend?

Being able to confide in your partner and share the same sense of humour is part of being in love. Many answered that their partner was their best friend.

"I like him a great deal as well as loving him. We often say we are each other's best friend. Outsiders describe our relationship as being best friends as well as lovers."

"Very much. Yes, he is my best friend, in a different way to my female friends. But we tell each other everything – we're very close."

"Definitely, definitely, definitely. He is the kindest, most considerate and thoughtful person I've ever known. I can tell him anything and everything. He makes me laugh, treats me with respect, supports me, understands my problems, shares my jokes, wipes away my tears. What more could you want from a friend?"

"He is definitely my best friend. He has stood up for me, and I only found out by chance later."

Some "best friends" were not as close, or as enthusiastic as others:

"He's too nice a person not to like, but is also incredibly annoying and frustrating. Only I see this, and friends and family think I'm melodramatic and a nagger about little things. He's my best friend, though."

"I like my partner as a person. Naturally there are things I would change and I'm sure he feels the same. Yes, I would say he was my best friend."

And in the following marriages friendship had dwindled or gone completely out of the window:

"I like him about 75 per cent, the other 25 per cent I tolerate but I wish it was different. He is not my best friend. A best friend to me is female, because women understand other women best."

"No, he is not my best friend. I like him sometimes."

"Not any more, no. I'm not very tolerant of all his faults. If I wasn't married to him I certainly wouldn't choose to get to know him."

"We are not friends at all, we just put up with each other, we are like black and white, anything I say he never agrees [with] and vice versa, he never shows his feeling, always been a man's man, goes out when he wants, comes home when he wants, it can be all hours, it would never enter his head to take his family out. It would be nice to have an arm round my shoulders, or a kiss on my cheek, this never happens. He calls himself the lodger. You might say, why didn't I leave, but where do you go with four sons? My husband is not very good or reliable at paying bills, so I don't think the maintenance would be paid. What is the alternative? There isn't one. We have a roof over our heads, just two separate worlds."

"I do not especially like his nature. Certainly never best friends."

Several women, including one who has been married for 48 years, write: "I love him, but I do not like him." What do they mean by "love"? Love without liking is not freely given; in the true sense of the word, it's not love at all, but a form of need.

There may be financial and social reasons for needing a partner you don't like, or the need may be a habit you feel powerless to break. If you feel "needy" and dependent, then even if you are living with someone you don't like, you become conditioned to the habits of the relationship, and they become the fabric of your life. Thus the woman who has been married for 48 years "loves" a man who has a terrible temper, throws things, is lazy and "says dreadful things, which he knows are not true, in order to hurt me as much as possible." She says she does not like his character, and if she were not married to him, she would not choose to get to know him.

This couple are in their 70s and part of a generation that found divorce less acceptable than we do today. That generation also took it more or less for granted that women would be dependent, which meant that, for the sake of respectability, they might be expected to put up with bad behaviour in silence.

Ask yourself what you really mean when you say you love your partner. Do you mean that you take delight in him? If you dislike him, you should make some changes in your life. Instead of seeing yourself as a victim of his unpleasant behaviour, you need to take responsibility for your own happiness. This means taking the power over your life out of your partner's hands and reclaiming it for yourself. As well as being more assertive, remind yourself of all the things you originally liked about each other. What activities did you enjoy sharing that you have since given up? Could reviving old interests bring back fun and laughter into your lives?

Q: Are you similar personalities?

Many more couples appear to be opposites rather than like each other. Introverts and extroverts pair well together, perhaps because each provides what the other lacks to form a balance. Perhaps having a partner is a way of rounding out your own character. Here are some typical answers:

"Not at all. I am the calming influence, easy-going and slow to lose my temper. My husband is much more volatile and claims I am the only person who can calm him down."

"No. He thinks before he speaks and is quieter. I talk a lot."

"No. He is quieter and quite easy-going. I'm more of a talker and have a short temper."

"No. I'm ebullient, vociferous, clumsy etc. He is quiet, measured, cautious, controlled, but not boringly so!"

"Not really, but we enjoy the same interests. He is quite quiet; I am quite noisy! He is more consistent and steadfast; I change my mind daily, hourly! He seems unemotional; I can be very emotional. We both have a sense of humour."

Among the couples who are alike, there are mixed feelings as to whether this is a good thing. For this couple the balance is perfect:

"My mum says we're like twins."

Two extroverts together can cause sparks to fly:

"Yes, and it can cause trouble! Quick-tempered and stubborn."

And introversion may be due solely to the shyness of youth, something that one partner grows out of, leaving the other behind:

"No. Total opposites now. When we met we were both very shy and timid. We seemed to have much in common then."

The characteristic most mention that they hold in common, even if they are otherwise opposites, is an identical sense of humour. As laughter is one of the great pleasures of life, resolving tension and creating an instant bond of understanding, it is essential that partners should be able to laugh at the same things — or if laughter is inappropriate, catch each other's eye and quickly look away!

 Q. What qualities and characteristics in your partner do you like best?

Sadly, too few men gave detailed answers for any conclusions to be reached about what characteristics they most appreciate in women.

At the top of the women's list came all the qualities that indicate a high level of personal involvement from their partners: responsibility, caring, gentleness, patience, reliability and consideration. It is often said that these "steady" attributes make good husbands but dull lovers. In fact, the women in this survey contradict that view. According to them, the men who are most deeply involved with their partners and with family life make the best lovers. This seems like straightforward commonsense. And why should responsibility at home be seen as dull when taking responsibility at work means promotion and is universally acknowledged to be exciting and desirable?

"Stability and reliability. Loving person. Very caring and protective towards me and our family. Excellent husband and father, very generous and supportive."

"His caring and considerate nature. As I have health problems I am no longer able to work. My husband considers it his responsibility to care for myself and our daughter. He is not at all chauvinistic and more than willing to share chores despite being the breadwinner."

"He is totally honest and genuine. Would never let anyone down if he could possibly help it. Very polite to other people (unless provoked in the car!) I trust him completely. He has a wonderful, very off-beat sense of humour. He's very affectionate and not afraid to let others know how he feels about me and the twins."

"The fact that he is fairly easy-going means that he is not worried about me doing more or less what I want. Knowing this, I rarely take advantage of him. He is generous and loving."

"He is very patient and understanding and rarely flies off the handle."

"He is responsible, a very good father, a good provider. Can be good fun, on holiday when not stressed with work commitments. He rarely criticizes me. I know he loves me and he tells me so."

"Honest, thoughtful, a brilliant lover, entertaining, sincere."

"Faithfulness. Sharing housework and childcare. Nursing during illness. DIY abilities. Above all, his acceptance of the fact that I inherited the lifelong care of my multi-handicapped sister after three years of marriage, when my father died. This care lasted 41 years – she lived with us for 30 years, disrupting the marriage. She died at 75 after 15 years in care."

25

And the following is a very interesting answer. It comes from a woman of 46 who has been extremely happily married to a man of 26 for six years.

"The ability to be highly responsible and thoughtful and yet tremendously wicked! It's a combination most men do not have – unlike most women. They're either responsible but boring, or fun but irresponsible."

Some women put their partner's sexuality at the top of their list:

"I like everything, really. Wanting to please me in bed before himself, although I've never had problems with sex."

"He is gentle and considerate when making love. He can be great fun, enjoys the children. Good at DIY and brings me flowers."

"Sexually we are very compatible, able to express our intimate feelings in sex. He has a great deal of trust in me, and appreciates my need for time on my own."

Others gave first mention to his sense of humour:

"Makes me laugh. Provides for our family."

"He's funny, caring, loving, generous and a good cook!"

"Sense of humour. Intelligence. Faithfulness. Agile mind, interested in many things."

Only a few put practical or financial skills in first place:

"His shrewdness over financial matters and his ability to talk about and share his feelings. His ability to relax in company."

"Good with figures, faithful, can be fun when tries, which is seldom, now."

"He is a good organizer. He gets things done once he starts. He is wonderful when I am ill. He is kind and gentle. He is a good timekeeper. He is gentle in bed."

"His willingness to solve practical problems. His cerebral approach."

Q: What habits, characteristics or peculiarities do you like least?

Again, there were not enough detailed answers from men to draw con-clusions about unlikeable female characteristics, but this was a question to which most women gave forthright answers. Together, they provide a picture of the '90s husband at his worst, though, strangely, violence was rarely mentioned in these answers. Other surveys show that 40 per cent of men are or have been violent towards their partners. Very few bat-tered wives have chosen to take part in this questionnaire.

A few negative qualities were mentioned in isolation: forgetfulness, moodiness, intolerance and inability to be punctual. Most of us know women with these failings, but the bulk of complaints against men cite characteristics and habits that cause women distress or irritation precisely because women so rarely share them. Most comments fall, broadly speak-ing, into two categories.

Men who remain stubbornly apart and refuse to communicate

Women operate naturally in networks of support. This is of course a generalization, and exceptions from public life and private experience spring immediately to mind, but it is one on which psychologists, broadly speaking, agree. It is impossible to say how much these qualities are inborn, and to what extent they are due to social conditioning, but on the whole, women are used to consulting, coming to an agreement, acting jointly for the good of the group. They take the lead when necessary, but do not usually like to act unilaterally. They find it incom-prehensible that men should act stubbornly against their own best interests or the interests of the family.

"He can be very stubborn and pig-headed – he tends to act first and think later. He won't stop for meals when working on home improvements. This gives him a migraine, which means that the whole family suffers. I find his habit of burping and farting noisily extremely irritating – I started him on the Hay system of eating and it really worked, but he won't stick to it now, even though I do."

"Stubbornness, inflexibility, not wanting any change in his life."

"Insensitivity! He is stubborn, can be bossy and a bit aggressive, not physically, though. Can be selfish with his time. Expects me to pander to him."

27

Men operate naturally in a competitive arena. This is another generalization on which psychologists agree; like the one about women, it's broadly borne out by personal experience. Watch boys and girls playing together and you will see how girls huddle and share secrets, while boys race and tussle and shout threats and challenges. Men jockey for position in a hierarchical world where it's important to be right, and important to come off best, which is why it's very difficult for them to back down.

In the high-pressure world of work, men excel at negotiating and bartering, and stubbornness often pays off. Women can also excel in these areas, of course, and have the additional advantage of being flexible. But in a domestic setting, which thrives on cooperation and harmony, a man's single-track mind and thrusting approach can be absurdly out of place.

It's humiliating for a man to be proved wrong or to be thwarted, because it strikes right at his masculine self-image, and when this happens at home, he may throw a tantrum or storm off rather than talk things through rationally.

"Has a short fuse sometimes. Drives aggressively. Not very intelligent."

"Obstinacy, lack of logic, flash temper over trivialities, inability to make decisions or take the lead, inability to give praise or pay compliments, takes me for granted, rarely takes me out."

"A very quick temper and the way he shouts and slams around if angry."

"Quick temper, occasional violence, withdrawal during arguments, very little touching, loving or caring physically when not having sex."

"He has a ferocious temper and cannot be reasoned with once riled. He takes ages getting round to talking about something seriously."

"He can be selfish. Very quick temper and he can rant on a lot. Makes a fuss at the slightest sign of illness. He farts a lot. (Can I write that?!)"

"Always twitching his foot. Won't argue. Always walks away, leaving me wanting to scream."

Surely these men are capable of having logical discussions with their colleagues at work, and don't fly off the handle or walk out as soon as they are presented with a complication? If they behaved at work like they do at home, their irrational behaviour would get them the sack.

Men don't need to have tantrums at work because the world of work is strictly hierarchical, and each person knows his place in relation to his boss and subordinates. Subordinates bring problems, and bosses solve them. Subordinates may question decisions, but the boss always has the final say. Authority is respected, and very rarely undermined.

Until fairly recently, there was a hierarchy at home, too, and men enjoyed a secure place in it: they were head of the household. Now, no such hierarchy exists. The domestic environment is about sharing: making joint decisions and taking joint responsibility. These are skills in which women excel, and men who can't tolerate their partners' excelling, and who take it as an affront to their masculinity, react by regressing into childish behaviour, throwing tantrums and storming off.

Women are going to have to encourage men to bring their diplomatic and negotiating skills home from the workplace and to apply them, cooperatively, in the domestic arena.

Another reason why men fail to discuss things with their partners is that the topic under question at home is often an emotional one. Men are not noted for being good at expressing their feelings, and this is another area in which women have had a great deal more practice.

Women have traditionally helped each other with childbirth, and looked after the very young, the sick and the dying. They care for the most vulnerable members of the community, and are familiar with weakness and suffering. For the most part of our history, men have been shut out of this area, indeed they have been trained to ignore it, and to deny weakness, pain and fear. Exploring their own emotions, which is what women are now asking them to do, makes them feel threatened. They feel more at home in the world of actions, or in silence.

"He refuses to talk about his feelings, and as a result, he has had an affair."

"Never being able to say sorry. He demonstrates his sadness by doing things, but he'll never say it."

"Sometimes not entirely truthful – this has improved with age! Moodiness – occasional sudden swings. Tendency to be secretive about some things, usually money."

"His quietness. He doesn't always share all his innermost thoughts as much as I would like. This can lead to misunderstandings."

"He constantly puts me down and has no respect for me. He can't communicate. He's a workaholic."

(See also page 38.)

Men who are slobs

Women are not generally slobs because of generations of training that has taught them consideration and care for the comfort of other people. Also, tradition, reinforced by modern consumerism, persuades women to beautify themselves and their surroundings to please men.

In a culture that, until recently, has revered them as the sole breadwinners and protectors of society, men have held a privileged position. Like their cave-dwelling ancestors, they have gone off during the day to bring back the bacon, and in return for their protection, the women have cooked and kept house. Today, even though most of the women in this survey share the responsibility for earning the family's keep, a large proportion of their partners still feel that it's part of the male birthright to be waited on.

But it's not just male arrogance and laziness that upsets women; it's what they see as the insulting behaviour that goes with it: deliberate farting and burping, picking at body orifices, being dirty. Spontaneous farting and burping are often funny, because they are a reminder that we are not as much in control as we seem to be. However, here we are talking about women who are hurt by *deliberately* antisocial behaviour, because they feel that their partners set out to provoke and disgust them.

There is an element of amusement in the first answer below – this woman gave her husband top marks for being sexy in the question above, and he is a very minor offender. But as you read down the list you see the woman's smile getting tighter, and a sense of panic gathering underneath it. Women don't really find slobs funny, because slobs offend against intelligence and sensuality; they hurt women at the core of their femininity.

"1. Hates shaving; 2. Can live in clutter and mess; 3. Clumsy; 4. Does most things slowly; 5. Occasionally indiscreet; 6. Picks his nails."

"Picking his nose, his fingernails, his sleep from his eyes, and flicking it. It drives me mad!"

"He picks his toenails and always leaves the wardrobe doors open. When he is annoyed he goes quiet and looks very menacing – UGH!"

"Making mountains out of molehills. Always looking to the past. Leaving toenails in the lounge – disgusting!"

"Smoking, snoring, smelly feet. When out with friends, not able to turn down a drink."

"Latterly he drank too much and became silly and argumentative. I found it hard to fathom what he really thought and felt. Aimless whistling. Leaving the lavatory dirty."

"He's untidy, leaving clothes around, he tries to 'act big', he breaks wind at inappropriate moments."

"When he leaves his towel on the floor! He doesn't wash the dishes sufficiently well. He likes the telly/football. He can get quite sulky, even quieter if he feels he has been wronged."

"He leaves his clothes lying everywhere and dirty glasses and cups. If he's tired he sometimes forgets that I am too and decides to take a rest and lets me do nearly everything."

"The fact that if I ask him to do something that he doesn't want to do, he will do it so badly that I won't ask him again!"

"He was very self-centred. He had a single person's life even when we were married. He was untidy and very uncaring."

"Smoking, drinking, not washing too often."

So why do men behave like slobs? One woman says her partner "tries to 'act big'". Being a slob does make a man bigger, in that it increases the space he occupies. The slob marks out his territory with the litter of dirty clothes and crockery that he leaves behind him, and one man leaves his mark on the lavatory. The slob makes himself bigger by projecting on to others an uncomfortable awareness of his presence – he sprawls in a space full of smell, noise and mess that his partner has to skirt around, and which he leaves for her to clean up.

A slob who lives alone inconveniences no one but himself – he can take up as much space as he wants. Solitary slobbish behaviour is often a sign of deep depression. The message it gives out is: "I don't care for myself." But slobbish behaviour in a shared home is a triumphant act of aggression. The message here is: "I don't care for *you*." It's a particularly male act, because space invasion is characteristic of male behaviour in a sexual as well as a territorial sense. In the act of sexual penetration, the male occupies the female's most intimate space. In the act of claiming territory, whether by conquering Ancient Gaul or leaving wet towels all over the bathroom floor, the man is saying who's owner, who's boss.

The phrase "acting big" also has sexual as well as territorial overtones. "Big", for men, is synonymous with "erect", with "virile". It's what being a man is all about. Men judge themselves by how big they feel or seem, and this causes anxiety, because it invites comparison. A man is made bigger by power and ownership, and in the male mind these are closely linked with sex — for instance, in the image of the seductive woman draped across the bonnet of the fast car. Men are highly competitive because they judge themselves by comparison, and for the same reason they are also terribly afraid of failure. One survey shows that most men are concerned about penis size, and wish theirs was bigger. According to psychologists, men who have persistent problems with erection often contemplate suicide. Doubts about virility and bigness — in the real sense and in the metaphorical sense — are responsible for the fragility of the male ego.

Some men are able to confront their vulnerability without fear, and have no need to act like slobs to prove how big they are. The women in this book are looking for the sort of man who doesn't judge himself by comparison with other men. They want someone who develops self-knowledge and can accept that his sexual and emotional response may be unpredictable and out of his control. The slob, on the other hand, "acts big" because he needs proof that he is big, and he needs proof because he has deep self-doubts that he can't bear to face. The slob who invades his family's living space with his mess, and his partner's eyes, ears and nose with his offensive habits, is the same man who refuses to discuss emotional issues that might reveal a chink in his armour; he is blind and deaf to any area where he might have to acknowledge himself as inadequate.

Slobbish behaviour often starts as a reaction to fatherhood. As we see on page 158 and subsequent pages, men who are not emotionally mature enough to accept the responsibility of fatherhood often behave with the jealousy of an elder child when a baby comes along and "usurps" their position, as they see it, of being number one in the affections and attentions of their partner.

These jealous men now have in front of their own eyes an example of what kind of behaviour their wives seem to "prefer": that of a helpless infant who makes smells and messes. In their subconscious minds they realize that the way to get their partner's attention is to rival the infant's demands, by regressing to infantile behaviour themselves. So they become slobs, and in their conscious minds they relish their "revenge": their partners' irritation and distress.

Being a slob has the desired short-term result, but a disastrous long-term effect on the marriage: one third of the women who contributed the comments above have already left their husbands.

Other things women don't like about men

Some female dislikes didn't fit into the two major categories above, but ought to be mentioned. The first and most important is smoking. Several women cited this as their major dislike:

"He smokes. Spends quite a lot of time on computers."

"His pipe smoking."

"Smoking, passing wind."

"The fact that he smokes occasionally!"

"Smoking. His 'Chinese' way of doing things – mechanically inept."

No one said so, but women must be worried for their partners' health and for the health of the other *passive* smokers in the family. Passive smoking is particularly damaging for pregnant women and for babies and, of course, polluting the atmosphere is just another way of enlarging your space and demonstrating who is in charge.

Next come a few irritations of the minor sort that most people have to suffer when they live together:

"Most irritating – and really quite trivial – is flicking back and forth between TV channels with the remote."

"Channel-hopping on TV, his lack of DIY and kitchen skills."

"Leaving the loo seat up, addiction to sport – nothing to jeopardize our relationship, though."

"He has an infuriating habit of rubbing his head, which he has done since childhood. He can be too generous giving his time to other people when we need him at home."

"Coughing to clear throat."

And finally, two women make the point that if one partner is sloppy and the other meticulous, they are bound to rub each other up the wrong way:

"When he is sensible and I want to be frivolous. His being a perfectionist sometimes annoys me because I have a slapdash approach. (I do wish he could dance!)"

"He is slapdash – the mediocre doesn't bother him. (That *really* gets me!) I always do everything to the best of my ability. Being a perfectionist is a fault in my character."

 How would you describe your partner as a lover?

A lot gave one-word answers, like "brilliant!" or "poor", but the longer answers set out below are more useful. They give a good idea of what qualities women appreciate most in a lover, and what they like least.

Women like men to be tender, imaginative, sensitive, uninhibited and totally involved. The men who answered this question liked the same things. Women like their lovers to be tantalizing and to take their time.

"The most tender, tantalizing, imaginative, sexy, considerate, loving dream any woman ever wanted. He's just gorgeous."

"Very tender, likes to give me satisfaction. After 30 years we still make the earth move for each other regularly."

"Adventurous, exciting, caring, loving, considers my needs, thoughtful."

"Very satisfying. Able to continue as long as I want to."

"Sensitive and slow. Takes his time and enjoys every bit! Very aware of what I want. Not worried about telling me what he wants too. Adventurous. 11/10!"

"Wonderful – caring, tender, exciting, passionate."

"Excellent! Never says no!"

"Perfect. He is gentle and caring. Very passionate and very aware of my needs as well as his own. Our love life is very enjoyable. Totally without inhibition."

"Very caring, gentle and loving. Very considerate of my feelings and my part in sex. We have lots of fun in bed. Nothing really embarrasses us."

"Lovemaking has improved over the years and we can both freely reach orgasm. He is a very gentle lover who longs to please. Has a good sexual appetite and is willing to try all sorts, e.g. making love in the snow in a pine forest, making love on the lawn in the summer. Always very considerate."

"Very tender and affectionate. Great understanding and appreciation of our needs for one another."

"Near perfect. He is very responsive to my needs and is very gentle and considerate – in fact he is not my idea of a typical man in this respect, and I am very lucky."

What both men and women like least in a sexual partner is detachment. Women who are detached are called unresponsive; men who have sex without involvement are described by their partners as selfish and mechanical – their wives say they are just "going through the motions". Women don't appreciate men who rush sex, or who lack imagination or confidence.

"Selfish, boring. I could predict exactly in what order he would do things. No imagination."

"Reasonably good, but too reserved. He is the only lover I have had who has *prevented* me from really being myself when making love! Sex is good, but he doesn't take time over arousing me, making love."

"My wife was brought up that sex was not nice, but she tolerated it because the Catholic Church said it was permissible after marriage."

"He is very caring and gentle, but with me, not at all adventurous. Sex in bed is all he'll do."

"Not very imaginative. Too quick. Boring. No foreplay."

"Average. He is caring, but sometimes it's wham-bam, thank you ma'am. I rarely reach orgasm, but that is all his fault."

"Routine. Tries to press the right buttons, usually succeeds, but I would enjoy a change of approach."

"I don't have any comparisons, but I feel he's just out for himself."

"He needs to be encouraged. He is easily aroused. He tends to be repetitive and has to be encouraged to try new things. He comes too early and doesn't wait for me."

"Unsure of himself. Lacks confidence. Considerate and tender at times."

Men who are boring and selfish in bed need to be initiated into the pleasures of eroticism and sensuality. A lot would benefit from curling up in bed with their partners and reading a good sex guide together. If you're worried that your partner might be offended by implied criticism, introduce your chosen book as a surprise, a curiosity, rather than a necessary remedial study aid.

The point of sharing it is that discussing what you read can be a good way of starting to talk more personally, exploring your own needs and preferences. Some people are shy of the vocabulary of sex, so use the words printed on the page in front of you to help. Talking personally about sex takes away embarrassment and is a liberating experience. And you'll find that it's much easier and more natural explaining what turns you on while you lie in each other's arms before making love, than issuing instructions like "Up a bit! Down a bit!" while it's happening. Talking intimately about what turns you on can in itself be very erotic, and eroticism is what is lacking in all the relationships described above.

Another way of educating your partner is to take more responsibility for lovemaking yourself. Show him the kind of slow, sensual lovemaking you would like. Don't allow him to participate at all; get him to concentrate entirely on the sensations in his body. Then allow your imagination and tenderness full rein. Hopefully, this will inspire him to want to do the same for you.

A woman of 77 describes a problem for which she says there was no professional help until it was too late for her husband:

"His lack of confidence and interest quickly turned to impotence. He believes sex is only for procreation and irrelevant otherwise. Never made love more than three or four times a year and *not at all for 45 years."*

Most men go through periods of stress in their lives when their libido is low and they can't get or maintain an erection. Usually, impotence is temporary and passes once confidence has returned in other areas of life, the more quickly if the couple give up trying to have sex for a while and just concentrate on cuddling and being affectionate and close.

Counselling is almost always helpful if the problem persists, because impotence is only very rarely caused by physical factors. Counselling will aim to discover the psychological root of the problem. A man might be unconsciously witholding sex from his partner because of some deep resentment or fear, for example. The counsellor will help the couple to work through these inhibiting emotions together, to take them out of the sexual arena so that they can be dealt with properly. He or she will then help the couple build up enough confidence and trust to resume sex.

Finally, here are two women who feel they are less highly sexed than their husbands:

"He is very virile and is more highly sexed than myself. Not as affectionate or gentle as I would like, but he does try to please. Rushes out of bed after."

"Predictable but considerate and understanding. I am not a sexually active partner, so sometimes fake desire out of consideration for him."

Some people (both male and female) suffer from inhibitions they don't even know they have. A fear of what might happen to them if they completely let go of themselves causes them to hold back, and often to play-act. Faking orgasm is a lonely business. Enjoying yourself in bed is about stripping away your protective layers – it's about being true to yourself. It can take courage to talk to your partner about what you don't enjoy in bed, because of course you're afraid of hurting his feelings, but the alternative is to make sex an endurance test and a lie. Since both the men above are willing to please, talking seems the right way forward. With a more gentle approach, their partners might find they are more highly sexed than they think.

Is the man in your relationship able to talk about his thoughts and feelings?

The fact that men find it difficult to talk about their emotions is one of the things that women like least about them (see page 27). There are, however, men who are in tune with their feelings and who are able to express them and share them:

"Yes, he's very spontaneous with his feelings. He will often ring me at work to tell me I'm beautiful or he loves me, or equally, he will tell me if he feels hurt. He is emotionally supportive, accepts my moods, joys, frustrations, PMT, the lot!"

"Very much so. I couldn't live with anyone with whom I was not emotionally intimate."

"He frequently divulges thoughts and feelings and we tend to feel [about] and think of the same things in the same way."

"Very supportive. Can diffuse my feelings of panic and crisis very quickly. Sometimes he needs coaxing to open up to what is really troubling him. The right words escape him sometimes when he wants to explain how he feels."

"Yes, he's very open about his feelings. Generally he's supportive – sometimes not in the way I want him to be, but that may be expecting him to read my mind."

In one case, a woman notes how things have improved since the family has grown and allowed them more time together:

"We talk more now, since our son has grown older. There was a period when we drifted apart because of the demands of the family."

For two other couples, a family crisis has enabled the man to open up with encouragement from his partner:

"He did tend to keep things bottled up once upon a time. But the last two years have been difficult due to lack of work, so I have encouraged him to talk about things more."

"Yes he can. We had a problem a few years ago following a bereavement when he shut himself off emotionally. It caused me deep distress and we have vowed never to let the same situation arise again. We now talk through our thoughts and feelings, good or bad."

Sadly, some men will talk freely only under the influence of alcohol:

"Not often. Usually when drunk."

Some men manage to provide their partners with emotional support, but cannot easily admit to their own vulnerability:

"He is emotionally supportive but finds it fairly difficult to talk about his thoughts and feelings."

"He doesn't talk about his feelings, but I know him well enough to tell when there's something wrong. Yes, he's emotionally supportive."

"He is not able to talk about his emotions easily. If he does, it's about something that was said or done months ago. As long as it doesn't relate to him, he's emotionally supportive."

And this man does his best, though his skills would be better suited to negotiating business deals, which is what he is probably used to, rather than to sharing feelings in a heart-to-heart:

"He is, but he takes ages and I get bored waiting for him to begin. He listens and understands well but demands exacting and precise conversation."

However, most women's answers to this question are an emphatic "No!" or "Never!" Men find talking about their feelings threatening, because it exposes them as vulnerable, and in the ordered and competitive masculine world, any vulnerability is attacked, like Achilles' heel. The result is disaster, or at least, diminished stature. So men are naturally defensive.

For women this means a bewildering and frustrating lack of communication, which they take to heart, being themselves used to sharing problems and commiserating over failures. Women whose partners can't talk about emotions can interpret their silence as a withdrawal of love.

"Absolutely not. He never talks about his thoughts and feelings. I wish he would."

"He doesn't reveal his worries and feelings much and ends up letting it get on top of him and shouting at me."

"No, I think he bottles these feelings up, then eventually issues an ultimatum without much discussion. Is afraid of opposition and analysis."

"He finds it very difficult to talk about his thoughts and feelings as I discovered when we had to have Relate [formerly Marriage Guidance] counselling about five years ago. He is not emotionally supportive."

For the following three women's husbands, *not* understanding emotion is a matter of male pride:

"He keeps his feelings bottled up, trying to be 'macho'. He hates it if I cry and can't understand PMT: 'Here we go again!' "

"He has no sympathy or understanding of women's emotional needs and believes that, for example, they cry to get their own way with a man. He *never* gives in to a woman, considering it a weakness."

"My husband *never* talks about his inner thoughts and feelings. He is very old-fashioned in that respect."

This woman sees how the problem can be passed on by example from one generation to the next:

"He is dreadful for bottling up his feelings because his parents are people who never show their emotions, and it is a struggle to reach him sometimes. It is the most frustrating part of our relationship, his inability to let go. I am a very up-front person and easily show how I feel."

And these women have come to the sad understanding that their husbands are just not equipped to deal with emotional issues:

"He will rarely talk about his feelings. He is not very emotionally supportive of me – I don't think he knows how to react in certain situations."

"He was only able to support me in practical ways."

Lack of communication is the single main reason for relationships breaking up, and for partners leading bitter, silent and separate lives in the same house. But if both sides understand the needs and fears of the other, this can open up a way for men to trust women more, and to liberate the emotions that have been suppressed.

Q: How would you like to change your partner? Can you change him/her?

Most agreed that it is not possible to change anyone other than oneself. However, your partner can change if he or she accepts your invitation and encouragement to do so. For some women in this survey, the way both partners changed and grew was one of the greatest satisfactions of marriage.

Four women give satisfied answers:

"I don't want him to change. I took on a complete package, good and bad. If he changed he would stop being the person I love."

"I would not like to change him in any way because he would not be his true self, the person that I know and love. I imagine he would be resentful if I were to try, and probably fight it, [thereby] achieving the opposite effect. I believe a partner can be sympathetic to your views and wishes without actually agreeing with them 100 per cent, and be willing to compromise. It would be very boring if we were all alike."

"He is not in a rut – he is developing in a non-specific way all the time. I like this maturing."

"I don't want to change him. Over the years he has mellowed and done things to improve himself, but this has been his choice and not anything I have tried to make him do."

This very positive acceptance of a partner as a whole person means that both have space to grow and change. It's a creative approach that stops a relationship from getting stale.

Three other women feel sadly neglected:

"Make him love and respect me. Make him dress better. Make him go on holiday with me and allow me to use the car."

"I would like him to make me his hobby. I would like him to be more thoughtful and caring, and a better lover."

"I would like someone who was more practical in the home and who would do jobs with pleasure. I would like someone who loved children and enjoyed their company and who would plan family days out and activities together. I would like to be able to chat rather than talk."

The majority issue a liberating invitation to the men in their lives to open up and relax and live more fully:

"I would like him to talk more openly about his feelings, his needs, his wants, his dreams, his fantasies. I cannot change him, only encourage more openness."

"I wish he had more spirit of adventure. Farmers are home birds. My husband is quite stubborn."

"I would like him to show more emotions, and give me a cuddle during the daytime. He doesn't change because he wants me to make the first moves all the time. I would like him to be more ambitious and to seek change."

"Make him more passionate and adventurous in lovemaking."

"Make him talk more about his feelings."

"Encourage him to show his emotions if he needs to. Make him think it's an OK thing for a man to do."

"I think with patience and more time, our sex life could improve. I would like it to be more fun and passionate."

"I would like to make him a bit more chatty."

One woman of 77 looks back on what might have been:

"I would have liked him to have ambition and [an] ability to earn well, and to make love, to *notice* me – take me out. He has to be dragged out except for his one interest, which is bowls. He has no interest in the world outside his home, whereas I have a lively interest in *everything*."

And many send out an urgent plea:

"To stop smoking."

There is nothing worse, if you don't smoke yourself, than breathing someone else's foul air in the knowledge that it could kill both of you.

Q: What is your idea of a real man?

The contributors to this survey declare themselves overwhelmingly in favour of the "New Man". A woman of 63 writes:

"Not a big protective hulk, but a caring considerate 'new' man. A man who is more like a woman."

The key difference that contributors understand between "new" and "macho" men is that new men have inner resources of strength, whereas macho men have to *act* tough to prove themselves all the time in competition against other men and in asserting arrogant superiority over women.

People who constantly need to prove themselves are fundamentally insecure. Women like men whose confidence and security comes from self-knowledge and acceptance. Inner strength and awareness enable a man to open up and care for, and be as much involved with, his family as his partner. If a man is always worried about his ego and the impression he is making on his peers, he will not have the depth of character or the energy to nurture intimate relationships.

"Someone who isn't afraid of what his male friends think and doesn't have to act irresponsibly to prove to them he is a 'real man'. Someone who cares about his family."

"Someone willing to turn a hand to anything without considering if it is someone else's duty."

"Totally caring and sharing, cares for home and kids as much as I do."

The characteristic women value most highly in men is the ability to feel, and to recognize and express their emotions.

"Someone who is in touch with himself, his feelings and is emotionally strong, but also vulnerable."

"A man who is manly, loving, honest, funny, caring, open and not afraid to show his feelings, generous and forgiving."

"Someone who knows he doesn't have to be a macho-man to show he is a man. Someone who is happy with himself."

43

"Someone who can face life on the same level as their partner, is not afraid to be seen doing family things, takes responsibility seriously, can give love and take love and share love with his partner without making conditions, and who can show emotion."

"Masculine. Popular with both men and women. Unselfish. Confident enough about himself to be able to show emotion. He doesn't have to be a 'he-man'. He doesn't treat women with contempt. He is not afraid to let people know he is in love."

"One who isn't afraid to show his feelings and consideration to his partner, especially in the company of others. I don't like macho men."

"Someone not afraid to show his feelings and able to cry."

Men who understand and express their emotions are liberated from generations of restrictive training that toughens them up and cuts them off from the sort of happiness and exuberance that fills the marriage of this next contributor:

"A man who has no problem about proving or being seen to prove his masculinity. A man who is at ease with his own convictions. A man who does what he feels is right. A man who rushes round pushing his baby really fast in her pushchair, because she likes it, and who doesn't worry about the stares. A man who can go into a busy shop and ask for a packet of Tampax Super with no embarrassment."

Of all the women who contributed to this survey, only two describe a "real man" in traditional terms. The first quoted below sees her husband as a true Tarzan:

"My husband. If stranded in the jungle he would soon make us a home, provide food and fight off any enemies."

And then there is a woman of 80, brought up in an age that abhorred and feared as depraved men who showed any softness or emotion:

"I hate to see evidence of feminine traits of any kind in my sort of man – especially 'arty types'."

Finally, these two women who are crushed in their marriages under domineering husbands protest that a "real man" would let them be themselves:

"Someone who sees me as an individual and doesn't try to run my life."

"One who isn't a chauvinist and lets a woman have her say."

The way this last woman expresses herself is disturbing, because the idea that a man should "let a woman have her say" presumes that he has the overall power to determine whether she should speak or not. In asking him to allow her to have her say, she is giving him control of her voice. She doesn't realize that she has just as much right to voice an opinion and be heard as her husband or anyone else on this planet, and because of this she is tacitly condoning and encouraging his male chauvinism.

Q. What is your idea of a real woman?

"Real" people, male and female, according to the contributors to this book, are those who know and accept themselves and are able to communicate their feelings.

"Someone who is in touch with herself and her feelings, and is emotionally strong but also vulnerable."

"The same things as regards love and emotions as a man, but also [one] who is strong, has her own views and is capable of doing things for herself and doesn't have to rely on men to get things done for her."

"Someone who is happy being herself. Too much is made of what men and women should be. It's more important to be content with yourself. If you don't want to be a wife and mother, then you shouldn't be pressured into being something you're not, and shouldn't be made to feel a freak because of it."

As the following contributors indicate, it is taking time for men to accept that women are their equals.

"The sort of woman men don't like! Confident, independent, capable."

"A woman who will stand up and be counted. Someone who will fight for her rights. Someone who doesn't use manipulative skills to get what she wants, but honest assertiveness."

"Individual and independent."

"Feminine with a mind of her own."

"Someone who can be strong yet feminine. A rock with a soft centre."

Some women still see homemaking as inextricably linked with femininity. While agreeing that home and family are important priorities, most contributors would bristle at this next entry:

"She is a homemaker, nurse, mother, cook, cleaner, counsellor, hostess. Supportive, tactile and a whore in the bedroom."

For this next man, unswerving loyalty is the most important quality in a woman:

"Someone who will gladly accept all you have to give, stand by you, and give you all she has to give, through thick and thin."

Two other women express very traditional views of what a woman should be – amazingly, physical beauty is their top priority!

"Pretty, slim, energetic. Someone who can turn her hand to anything, a good cook, good at needlework, artistic. Willing to help with physical chores, strong in mind and body. Loving, caring, gentle, good with children and old people."

"Beautiful, loving, caring, understanding."

These last contributions show how slowly some women are emerging from a view of themselves taken from the traditional male standpoint, where women are judged for their supportive abilities and decorative appearance, and not as personalities in their own right with the potential for fulfilment.

 Do you think men or women are the stronger sex? Why?

Male and female contributors agree almost unanimously that women are the stronger sex. The only area in which men might have the edge is in physical strength, but even that is disputed:

"Men are more single-minded, and they have stronger muscles. Women are better at understanding others' problems."

"Women – certainly physically."

It needs to be pointed out here that men, traditionally society's bread-winners, are getting a rough deal in the 1990s because unemployment is denying them what used to be their prime function in family life. The disorientation that men are suffering has contributed to the recent alarming increase of male suicides.

On the other hand, women, who have always been strong in home and family life, are extending their prowess into the world of work.

Here are some of the reasons why women are felt to be the stronger sex:

"Women are more independent, they seem to understand people more, have more compassion and are less selfish. Women seem to cope better and have fewer hang-ups. I know this is generalizing, but I find it to be true of most women I know."

"Women carry the burden of the whole family in terms of organization and management."

"Women really are in control of things. They see beyond the immediate and can discuss things properly."

"Women can live without men but not vice versa. They need women to care and look after them."

"Women are stronger. When there's a problem, my partner just buries his head and goes to bed."

"I think women are stronger because they have to deal with so much in life – I am doing the role of two people by myself. They are more emotional than men and so deal with life's problems right at the core, not on the surface."

"Women seem to have higher pain thresholds. We were brought up to bear pain, grit our teeth, not to complain – it's ingrained. But yes, I feel we are stronger, because when something happens, we set out our stall and get on with it. In fact, figures show that more men than women commit suicide. It takes a lot of guts to do it, but in the end it's the coward's way out."

"I think women are more open and emotional and therefore deal with situations better. I also feel you get more support from a female friend than a male would from a male friend, because females tend to be more honest with each other.

Women have more ways of dealing with situations than men do. Within my marriage we have done things that my husband said he'd never do, decorated with colours he said he'd never use, gone places he said he'd never go, etc. – and he's thought it was his idea."

It is interesting that the particular skill of persuasion described in this last entry is often labelled "manipulative" by men who unwittingly succumb to it. When they see the same skill in themselves, they call it "diplomacy". However, men are more likely to blow their cover afterwards by crowing over their success. More women should enter the political arena, where their discretion and tact, allied to their skills of persuasion, could make a valuable contribution.

The next two entries smart with a hurt that is turning into disdain:

"Women. They run the home, have the kids, and mother their partners. Men will always be boys; girls are born women."

"He is physically stronger and he's proved it. Women have an inner resource – mine is being saved for a rainy day!"

The next three contributors believe that men are stronger precisely because of their failings in the emotional sphere.

"Men because they are physically stronger and emotionally able to shut off."

"I think men are the stronger sex because generally they are not as emotional as women. I am too emotional, which undermines my confidence, which in turn makes me indecisive."

"Men are – they have the earning power, and they don't have periods."

Finally, one contributor sets the relative strengths of men and women in context and looks in hope towards a future in which men will be able to acknowledge their vulnerability, and enjoy the benefits of liberating their emotions.

"Women are stronger emotionally because they have been conditioned throughout the ages to confront and deal with the emotional issues in life: care of the family, the young, the sick and the dying. However, the emphasis is changing. With more women at work and unemployment, more men are having to cope with child-rearing and family care. The gap between the sexes is much narrower than in my mum's day.

Emotional strength comes with being allowed to discuss weaknesses in one's own character and situation. Men are more able now to own up to their emotions without feeling that vulnerability makes them less masculine. Once men truly open up and are able to demonstrate their feelings honestly without worrying about their macho image, then they will reap the benefits that women feel now by being allowed to be emotional. It's safe, it's an outlet, and it's OK."

LIFE TOGETHER

Contributors get to grips with the mechanics of marriage and speak their minds about everything from housework to sexual jealousy. In the practical sphere, *sharing*, and in the emotional sphere, *trust*, are seen to be the cornerstones of life together. A union built on sharing and trust provides security, and a springboard from which each partner can go out into the world. The fact that women spend twice as much time as men on domestic duties is seen – unsurprisingly – to be a major reason for women's dissatisfaction with marriage. It helps explain why three quarters of all divorces are initiated by women.

 What are the pleasures and benefits of being married, or in a stable long-term relationship?

For both sexes, the good things about being a couple are the same: they enjoy the love, companionship and security that marriage provides.

The first answer gives an inspiring view of marriage:

"Freedom. Freedom to be yourself, develop yourself, alongside someone who loves you and accepts you and whom you can trust totally, and with whom you can share everything in your life. This gives you a springboard from which to go out into the world."

This woman, who is 46, has been with her 26-year-old partner for six years and her answers show a dimension of fulfilment that others rarely experience or even imagine.

Here is another stirring answer:

"Having a reason for everything we do. Seeing pleasure in my husband – knowing he is happy makes me happy. Having someone to share with and make plans with."

A woman in a passionate 11-year marriage starts off a series of answers about love and companionship:

"Getting to know him better. I would like to get inside him."

"He is my friend – he's always there when I need him – hopefully we will grow old together – memories – no one can ever take them away."

"We are so comfortable with each other. We think alike and often have the same thoughts at the same time. We like each other as well as love each other. We feel complete when we are together."

"You can always be yourself – you don't have to put on a front."

"Having a companion, having someone to talk to who understands you. Having a friendly face to come home to and a hug waiting."

"Loving, warmth, sharing, caring, not being alone."

"Belonging, security, sharing things, company, fulfilment. Bringing children into a safe and loving environment."

"Having someone of your own to relate to. I had an almost telepathic knowledge of some aspects of my husband's mind."

"Feeling of belonging. I enjoy sharing the same name."

"I always have an understanding listener. I enjoy regular safe sex. I feel happier than when I was single."

Interestingly, though some contributors are worried about the effect of AIDS on their children's generation, this was the only mention of personal danger from sexual disease. It seems that married people feel somehow immune from AIDS, yet this survey and others indicate that around three-quarters of married people have other sexual partners. Do all adulterers use condoms?

These following answers concentrate on security:

"Growing together and stability. Being able to make long-term plans with confidence."

"Commitment to family, financial security. Someone with whom to share thoughts, feelings, problems."

"Feeling of security. Being able to be completely yourself. A close friend nearby always. Having someone to come home to. Sharing things together."

"Having someone to turn to in times of need. Security."

"Sharing things. Having someone there to rely on in all sorts of situations. Security."

And a man of 77 sums it all up in one word:

"We have what you would call in Cockney language, SPARK."

All these answers show that personal rapport — love, friendship, trust — is the key ingredient for making marriage work. This was not always so. As recently as the 1950s, marriage was measured not from within, in terms of personal happiness, but from without, in terms of success. One woman in this survey still sees marriage in terms of social standing:

"We have a good life, a nice house, lots of holidays, a good social life. We understand each other, have a great deal of respect and are proud that we have stayed the course."

 ## *Q.* What are the drawbacks of being in a marriage or long-term relationship?

A number of contributors said there were no drawbacks to their marriages at all — except the fear that their partners might die first and leave them to spend their last years in loneliness. For one woman the drawback was that no matter what promises you made, there could never be a guarantee of stability in any long-term relationship.

For those in bad marriages it can be difficult to name anything that's not a drawback:

"His character. Violence. Lack of caring. Plus loss of independence, cash, time to myself and to share with my friends."

The drawback most often mentioned was loss of independence and autonomy:

"Always having to consider another person before you act. Not always able to have a bit of space and time alone if you need it."

"Losing certain freedoms, having to confer about most things. Lack of choice sometimes."

"Sometimes it annoys me when I hear myself saying 'we' all the time and never 'I'."

"Not being able to choose your own curtains and carpets. Having to discuss everything. Not having control of how money is spent when he is away."

"The demands of other people on your time, e.g. inlaws. The feeling that sometimes you take on more than one person."

"Loss of freedom."

"No time for myself."

"Trying to keep your own identity."

One woman offers her solution:

"Having your own space when you need it can be a problem from time to time. I've found the best way to get round this is to do what I want when I know my partner is going to be out, or if that isn't convenient, just to be honest and say I need some time on my own for a while. I'm not specific, but I say how long I will be so he is not left 'hanging'."

And another concludes:

"You have to share and compromise but this is not a drawback when you count the benefits it brings."

The other common complaint was boredom. These are marriages where the spark has definitely died:

"Domesticity – the fun runs out."

"Sex becomes another job to do and unexciting. You get to know each other too well."

"Familiarity really does breed contempt."

"Things can get slightly boring. Too much routine. Individuals get taken for granted."

"Boredom. Being taken for granted. Sexual complacency and boredom."

"Sleeping with one person for ever (it's a long time)."

If your marriage is in a rut, you need to do something about it, urgently, before it slithers into the past tense. You need a change from routine – a break without the kids, preferably in a new setting, some mutual treats, and some deep talking to work out why you are still together, and what the prospects are for getting closer and staying that way.

 How satisfying is your sex life together? How has it changed?

Sex is the most intimate means of communicating our feelings, and couples whose feelings for each other are continually deepening and developing become increasingly finely attuned to each other's sexuality.

In the Bible, when people have sex, they are said to "know" each other, and this is not a euphemism but a good description of the potential of making love. Getting to know each other can be an ongoing process as you both change and grow, as long as your relationship thrives on an open exchange of feelings. With knowledge comes trust, and in an atmosphere of acceptance, inhibitions fall away, sex becomes more fulfilling, and your relationship gets better all the time.

"Very satisfying. Has more meaning and is more pleasurable than it was in the beginning. Because we are comfortable with each other and have no inhibitions we are able to please each other. There is no embarrassment."

"It has improved a lot over the years. We are both adventurous and he encourages my sexuality. He has never hidden the fact that he desires me."

"Very satisfying. It's more experimental than in earlier years."

"Extremely satisfying. Sex seems to get better as time goes by."

"Very satisfying. We're much more adventurous in our 40s than we were in our 20s."

"My sex life with my husband has improved because I feel totally at ease with him and he spends time on me and is gentle."

"Drastically! We make love a *lot* less, but it is far more fulfilling and enjoyable for *both of us*."

"Sex is now less frequent, but is still as passionate, and probably more fulfilling emotionally, as it's founded more deeply on love than on the sexual drive and emotions of youth."

"I find it exciting that sex makes babies."

For two passionate couples the only frustration is that they can't make love often enough:

"It's very satisfying, though I would like more sessions. It's changed from being fairly exciting to being very exciting. In the beginning we were happy touching and progressing to the sex act. Then taking longer, caressing and trying different positions; now we find that lovemaking is different every time."

"Our sex life is satisfying, and has matured greatly. Whereas in the early days we were doing it all the time and the ultimate goal was orgasm, now we enjoy it all – no hurry, just greedy! We still have a good quick session now and again because we fancy good quick sex. Our two children and full-time jobs make us very tired – often we fall into bed too tired for anything. Or we might start foreplay and fall asleep half way through! We don't get hung up about it. We just laugh. We could do with sex more often – we're both agreed on that."

The next woman has been with her partner since she was 16. Though her sex life is good, her sexual self-image has suffered since motherhood, and she seems to be looking outside her marriage for reassurance:

"Our sex life has improved. We both work at doing things the other finds pleasurable. We enjoy experimenting with positions. We both enjoy a long lovemaking session in the bedroom, but sometimes it can be just as exciting having a "quickie" in the lounge or kitchen. I also enjoy wearing clothes that my husband finds a turn-on. We have found watching a blue movie exciting too. Although we both enjoyed sex quite quickly after having both children, I dislike not feeling sexy because I'm too tired or working night duty.

I sometimes wish I could be flirtatious or that someone would make a pass at me. This is not because I am unhappy or that I wish to jeopardize our relationship, or even that I would take it further; I think it is because sometimes I wish to be seen as a woman first and not just a mum."

Another woman finds that the physical experience of pregnancy and childbirth has given her a much stronger sexual identity:

"Our sex life has improved as we have matured. I'm more relaxed about letting go since the children were born."

For some, the risk of pregnancy and the whole business of contraception takes the spontaneity out of making love. Two women describe how much better they feel now the risk has been removed:

"It's got better. My hysterectomy six years ago really improved things – that and unbroken sleep! Possibly less passionate, but more fun – and comforting."

"Seemed to go through peaks and troughs. Since my husband had a vasectomy it seems to have evened up and become regularized. It is really good – much better now than it ever has been, relaxed and very enjoyable."

A chaplain gives a robust piece of advice:

"Still as active as ever! But my wife always has one week off during periods. That should be mandatory in relationships. Does much to give partners a rest and renew desire."

Finally, one couple show how they are passing on their healthy open attitude to sex to their teenage daughter:

"Our sex life has always been healthy. There is as much desire for sex now as there was 20 years ago. My 15-year-old daughter said: 'You two get worse as you get older.' But we said: 'Is it that we are getting worse or you are getting more sexually aware?' She agreed that she is more sexually aware and that our fooling around in the kitchen etc. has always been an element of our feelings for one another."

Sex and parenthood

Though some women can hardly wait to resume their sex lives after childbirth, others may take months to heal after stitches. Scar tissue can make intercourse very painful, restricting a couple to oral sex and masturbation. The other major reason for reduced sexual interest and activity when there are babies or young children to be looked after is sheer exhaustion.

"Reduced dramatically! Mainly due to tiredness on my part and worries that the children might interrupt."

"Not very. It used to be wonderful, but it eased off after the baby, then we lived with my parents, which turned me right off. So far the urge has not overtaken me."

"It's good, but has changed a lot since the twins were born. We both feel very tired at the end of the day. My body still hasn't recovered after nine months!"

"When sex does happen it's very good, but as we have seven children it doesn't happen as often as it used to."

"Sex was good and often until we had our little boy. I would say that children, not being married, make the difference."

"Wot sex life? Before, we had sex 3–4 times a week. Now it's about once a month, rushed, before they wake up."

"Lessened. All our energies are centred around the girls and we have to make time for ourselves when neither of us is too tired to bother – but it is still good."

It's important not to let things get on top of you, and to make time to be alone together. Above all, don't stop being physical with each other: let your love and affection be part of the fabric of your life, and express your feelings in ordinary ways. This couple's children are growing up in a secure and loving environment:

"We have sex less frequently, because of exhaustion. If at all possible, we find the best time is during the day or after an early evening bath together. We cuddle a lot, which I find very reassuring, and it's acceptable in front of the children."

The good news for parents is that things do improve. If exhaustion and lack of time and privacy have put a complete stop to your sex life, you may be worried that you will never recover your libido and drift apart. These accounts show that, as long as you continue to be close in other ways, sex may eventually be even more fulfilling.

"When we first had a sex life together we couldn't get enough of each other.

When our son was born, it fizzled out almost completely. We now have a wonderful sex life."

"Loss of libido after babies due to tiredness, poor body image, lack of self-confidence. Now it's brilliant again, so less bickering and disagreement. It's very up in a calm relaxed way – we have time to enjoy each other again."

"Obviously, having teenagers, it cannot be spontaneous. Sometimes when we are alone it's very hard to turn on just because the house is empty. But having now matured, when we make love, we both have the experience for it to be ten times better than when we first met. Also, having such trust in someone else."

"It became nearly non-existent for several years with two small over-active girls, but as they have grown, it has flared up again, with not exactly a vengeance, but with loving and tenderness. After a vasectomy no fear of pregnancy helps also."

"I had quite a lot of stitches and also developed a ridge of scar tissue. That coupled with the fact that I was breastfeeding, which makes you drier anyway, and I felt permanently tired, did not make it a very good time sexually. I found it quite painful for a while and it took a good year for things to improve. We don't make love as often, but it's more fulfilling when we do."

"It just keeps getting better and better. We've always been able to talk about sex, and we spend hours talking about it, and as much time as we can doing it. Physically it's much better for me since having the children, although if you'd asked me before I'd had them I'd have been just as happy. On the minus side, it's the time factor with young children, and the weekend lie-ins as they used to be seem a memory of heaven – I can't believe that we actually used to spend all day in bed! We don't have the quantity of sex that we used to have, but the quality is much better, although when we were first together I used to think that it couldn't get any better, but it just seems to. Now our daughter is a little older, we're enjoying finding out about each other all over again, and we've definitely found my G-spot since I've had babies!"

Finally, here's a woman whose sex life has decreased, but whose marriage feels just as loving as it always did:

"What sex life? (Joking!) But it's definitely tailed off. We were like kids in the first year or two of marriage – it was great experimenting and we had few inhibitions. It was great to be married, and to be officially allowed to do it. But over the last five years it has tailed off. There has been as much as two months in between! But there is far more affection. Sex is nothing like as big a part of our lives as it used to be. When it happens, it is lovely, but we have both said we don't need the sex act to prove that we still love each other."

"It's not quite as good as it could be"

For some, passion and intensity has faded, though sex is still enjoyable. One woman thinks of several reasons why this might be, but does not examine her feelings for her husband. In fact, she lost interest as soon as they were married. Perhaps it was the "forbidden" that attracted her so strongly.

"The intense sexual pleasure and excitement that we both experienced before we married never happened thereafter. That is not to say that we have not enjoyed our sex life since, but only that the pleasure has not been so intense, and for many reasons.

Lack of privacy is the main passion killer. Firstly, living with his parents. Then, when the children were teenagers and sleeping in an adjoining room or going to bed at the same time or later than us. When they switch on the bathroom light next door it's like switching off the passion button.

After three children, a woman's muscle tone is affected and that can result in a decrease of sexual pleasure. Going back to work full-time is tiring and means less energy for sexual pursuits.

Sex becomes something to enjoy when the kids are all out of the house on a Saturday afternoon."

The next five contributors describe complex reactions to sex. Though they are brightly cheerful about it, there is the troubling feeling that something crucial is missing. These women are bewildered, and on the way to expressing their frustrations. Perhaps writing down their feelings helped.

"Occasionally sex is very good, if I dare to be a bit different, but usually it's just OK. He feels content that his sex drive isn't as strong as mine. We often misunderstand each other. I feel rejected, he feels pressurized, he worries how I will react if he does certain things. In fact, underneath, we both often want the same thing! We don't make love as much as we used to."

"It is slowly recovering after his affair, but I need more sex and more variety than he claims to want. I still lack real trust in him as a lover."

"It's good. It's less regular than it was. I would like sex every day but he says he is too tired. He can be a wonderful lover when he's had a few drinks, as this slows his performance down."

"Sexual intercourse has always been very good indeed. We nearly always climax together, but foreplay and after is non-existent, partly due to my husband's lack of hygiene care."

"We have a good sex life, in fact. It has got better over the years. Although I can't remember the last time he said he loved me, and I'm not sure I love him anyway. He never shows his feelings."

"It's not satisfying at all — it's practically non-existent"

For around a quarter of all contributors, sex was a rare or unpleasant occurrence, or else had stopped altogether. About half this group was over 50 and more or less resigned to celibacy. Resigned or not, these are the people whose marriages have lost their spark.

"Our sex life has faded away. In the past four years we have not really had a sex life at all. We are now resigned to celibacy."

"No sex for me since 1965."

"We have our own rooms and only occasionally sleep together. I am not too bothered."

"Sexual activity virtually nil, though we are good friends and are able to talk. Both of us have come to accept this state of affairs, though I find it frustrating at times."

For most, sex had tailed off gradually, but some were incompatible from the start:

"Very poor sex life throughout marriage. Both very inexperienced and did not learn much until we both had lovers."

"I don't think my husband and I were ever sexually compatible. I have enjoyed sex much more since I have been divorced, although at the moment I don't have a partner."

"I can only remember one example in 32 years where my wife was passionate in lovemaking."

This last man is retired, and locked in a bitter and loveless marriage, from which he feels powerless to escape. There is a feeling that he has taken part in the questionnaire as a means of letting off steam. He describes vividly the stifling narrowness of their life together, and the "veil of silence" that descends, often without warning and sometimes for days on end, when his wife is displeased. You can almost hear their knives and forks clattering in the hostile chill that hangs over the kitchen table. Over the years she has refused all his attempts to talk about sex, "a taboo subject", and now immerses herself in radio and TV, deliberately cutting off all channels of communication. She keeps a neat house. He takes refuge in his vegetable garden, or in a book.

Divorce is probably unthinkable for this couple, and there may be other dynamics holding them together. They keep up a very respectable appearance for the sake of the outside world. It is certainly a blessing that younger generations place more importance on personal happiness than on appearances, and that separation and divorce offer a realistic alternative to married misery.

There is always anguish when one partner wants to have sex more than the other. Is the one who withdraws and refuses to talk about it having an affair?

"My husband is not as interested in sex as he once was and this has caused me a lot of unhappiness."

"Our sex life is not as important as it should be. My partner is not keen to discuss or change this."

Love and respect have died when a woman begins to see sex as an obligation rather than as something she can't wait to do.

"It became a duty to fulfil. I was always very tired, which didn't help."

"Sex is rare – perhaps twice a month. No foreplay, no romance, no emotion. It's something I do because I feel I *owe* him. I imagine it's Alan Rickman, Mel Gibson etc."

"It was very good initially. After the age of 50 I hated it. I had no need of it and I resented him because his need was a physical one. I expect I disappointed him a lot. I 'obliged', but guess he knew it was 'duty'. It was not his fault. I felt fat and old and ugly, but he said he loved me still."

In this last very sad case, the husband left and now has another partner. It seems as though the contributor's poor self-image may be due to her menopause. It is possible that an understanding doctor could have helped. Hormone replacement therapy (HRT) can hold back the ravages of age, stabilize the swinging moods and depressions caused by hormonal upheaval, and minimize the sexual discomfort that comes with vaginal dryness.

Here is another woman who has not felt the benefit of HRT:

"Changed since the menopause. I found it painful, which deterred me, and now he is older I do not find him attractive."

One man of 77 and two women, one in her 70s and the other in her mid-50s, testify to the fact that sex can be enjoyed long after the menopause:

"110 per cent satisfying, but it has slowed down since we were 60."

"Very. We were still making love up to a few months before he died of stomach cancer, aged 67."

"My husband is 65. Our sex life has continued to be excellent, apart from a few months during pregnancy and after the birth when it was non-existent – we have made up for it since."

For many in a sexless, loveless marriage, the obvious step is to divorce:

"We divorced. There was no sex life for six months prior to separation, and prior to that, sex was something to be got through. I felt it wouldn't have mattered to him who was in his bed."

The following two women describe the change a loving caring partner can make:

"It got worse. His needs didn't match mine. His sex drive dropped to two or three times a month, and when I suggested sex it was a shock to him. I began to think the fault was mine. This feeling stayed with me, getting worse for about 12 years. I wondered if I was fat, unattractive, something wrong after childbirth. These feelings only disappeared two years after my divorce, with lots of reassurance from my new partner."

"With my second husband our sex life is very fulfilling and I feel my sex life has improved from one of mechanical sex to one of making love."

This woman has found happiness with her lover:

"We have not had sex for two years. My husband accepts this. He does not know I am having an affair. I felt for many years that my marriage was not fulfilling me and that there was not a closeness. Having met another man with whom I can relate, I realize how empty my marriage is. My new partner is my friend. We share interests and have much in common and consequently our sex life is a totally different experience – a loving one – compared to that with my husband."

Finally, three women are struggling courageously to improve their marriages with the help of counselling:

"After my husband's affair, he abused me for seven years. I then stopped sex altogether for two and a half years, and with the help of counselling was then able to start again on my own terms, i.e. not allowing myself to be abused."

"I allowed myself to be abused, believing my husband that I was the one with the problems. Counselling has shown me [that this is not the case]."

"Not very satisfying for either of us, at the moment. I am not very responsive (I do try, but my body won't listen). He feels he is pestering. I am seeking professional help. He is very patient."

The last couple's future is still in the balance, though if they part, the impression is that it will be with greater self-knowledge and the acceptance that they are making the right decision together. All too often when people break up, they have to work through the reasons for incompatibility afterwards alone, which can cause dreadful bitterness. This next couple's honesty will be their healing, whether they stay together or part:

"We have talked it all through and made more time just for us, tried to get our privacy back and get more interest in our sexual life."

If one of you is financially dependent on the other,
how do you feel about this?

Over half the women in this survey are working mothers who did initially take time off to look after their family (see also page 106). They find it satisfying to share financial responsibility.

"We have both been in the position of depending on the other financially. Prior to both situations we discussed the possible outcomes before volunteering to be dependent on the other. We are very supportive of each other, with no problems in this area, though money has been in short supply. We can always talk it out."

"We both equally need each other's salary. We pay the bills with one and live off the other."

"We both work in reasonably well paid jobs now. I left work to have a family and he supported me for several years. I went back to work when we both felt the time was right. We have joint finances which we are mostly both happy about."

One third of the remaining contributors is retired; the others are currently financially dependent on their partners while they look after their young families (see also page 150). Hardly any see this as an ideal state of affairs.

"Frustrating, but if you want to be a full-time mum, something has to give!"

It's often easier to give than it is to take:

"My husband likes being the provider, but I feel uneasy. When we were both working I did not see my earnings as 'my' money, but for some reason I now sometimes see my husband's earnings as 'his' and am reluctant to spend on myself."

"My husband feels the money he earns is ours. I feel it's his and I want my own financial independence, but I am at home with three small children at present."

"At first I didn't like it. I felt I should be responsible for everything at home and make my contribution. But because of my health problems this is not always possible. My husband prefers me not to work. He likes to be the breadwinner and to be responsible for us."

"I am dependent on my husband and I hate it. He has no problem with this and doesn't understand my feelings."

Even if your partner is generous, it can feel like freeloading to spend money that he earns on yourself.

"He is happy for me to stay dependent, but I have returned to work part-time and feel better that I can at last spend some money without guilt or worry."

Several women worry that taking time out of work to bring up children is doing permanent damage to their earning power. How would they ever get back into a career if they were suddenly left on their own?

"I'm financially dependent on him. He's never objected. I worry sometimes what would happen if we split up. It would be difficult for me to earn a decent living as I have been at home for years raising children and have no career of my own."

For some women, financial dependency is a source of bitterness against their partners.

"I am financially dependent on him. I feel trapped and resentful."

The next woman works for the family business, but is not a business partner. It feels like unpaid labour because her husband has total financial control and her time and skills are not rewarded with proper recognition or a wage packet.

"I feel very strongly about this – I really regret being financially dependent. I have played a very supportive role doing all the farm accounts (I am a qualified farm secretary) but have never been paid."

If the frustration of the non-earning wife is directed at her husband, neither will enjoy her dependency.

"Neither of us likes this situation, and I have always tried to earn a little so that I can have some money of my own."

Earning your own living gives an increased sense of identity and self-respect. Women who have no income of their own are often reluctant to spend "selfishly", as they see it, on their appearance, and this may reinforce a low self-image. It's easy to wear the same dowdy old clothes all the time if you're at home doing messy jobs, and to forget what a boost it gives to your ego to enjoy looking good. If your self-esteem is low, you are not likely to be feeling very sexually confident.

One woman who feels impotent in bed and unable to respond to her partner makes a direct connection between earning power and sexual potency, and fantasizes that if she were a big wage earner, she would overpower him.

"At eighteen when pregnant, extremely grateful, then realized the treasurer is the more powerful. I would love to have his earning power, but know that this would affect our relationship drastically. I would be too powerful for him."

Interestingly, there is also a connection between earning power and potency in the case of the 77-year-old woman whose husband has been impotent for 45 years. She worked to keep the family afloat all through her married life, except for the first seven years of motherhood. She writes: "I cannot imagine what it would be like to be totally supported by one's husband. My husband's salary – £3,000 at its peak – covered the basics only." She is married to a man who is ineffectual and disengaged – the opposite of dynamic. Earning power and sexual potency are both dynamic, and they feed confidence into each other.

The next woman's husband isn't overpowered by her earning power. Indeed, it may be part of her attraction:

"I earn the most and have done all along. So long as we don't go nuts, we try not to watch the other's spending."

However, it's not how much you earn that counts, or no woman would ever reach her true sexual potential – women have only 73 per cent of the earning power of men! What's important is the feeling that you can make your own way in life, and do your job well.

Unemployment creates emotional as well as financial strain, and re-dundancy hits hard at self-respect:

"Yes, he is dependent on me and I hate it. I wish he'd get a job soon. Life would be easier as well as happier."

Unusually, in the following household, it's the husband who is finding his wife's dependency difficult to adjust to:

"I have always worked, but I have just given up to have our second child. I feel happy about this, but I feel my husband resents it a bit – though he hasn't actually said so. He makes a point of saying that he bought this or that!"

And finally, here are two examples of double standards. The second shows that women can be as guilty as men in this respect.

"The only time I was dependent on my ex was after my daughter was born – he actually said he resented keeping us and spending all his money on prams etc. I supported him for some time before this and he considered what was mine was his. I was the one who kept the household accounts, and if he drew out large sums of money he would flatly refuse to explain what he spent it on, but I had to explain all my bills."

"I wouldn't mind if I were financially dependent on him if he were generous, but I wouldn't want to support him."

 How has the recession affected your relationship?

Many said the recession had affected their lives though for some, there was nothing new in being hard-up.

"We've always had to be careful with money."

"Fewer biscuits but no real change – we have been hard-up before."

Dwindling resources mean fewer outings, and more organization and worry.

"We had to sit down and work out the priorities. It has made things difficult at times. Many pleasures such as holidays have been put on hold."

"Things have got harder. We stay in more."

"It has affected us. I have to work to provide extras for us and the children."

"More pressure, worry, anxiety, inability to plan for the future with the threat of redundancy."

For some, it has meant a drastic and distressing change of lifestyle.

"It has meant my husband has had to go abroad to work and this has caused us both distress. We hate being apart. Fortunately we are both strong enough to cope, but we don't like it."

"It has put a lot of pressure on us as my husband was made redundant."

This man is unemployed and has to take odd jobs where he can find them:

"I feel inadequate compared to others. I resent doing shitty work for shitty pay. My life is now generally miserable. I feel deeply frustrated and have suicidal thoughts. Miserable."

Living with depression and bleak future prospects puts an enormous strain on a relationship, and sex will be the obvious first casualty.

"My partner was made redundant two years ago. This really knocked his confidence and he has been depressed ever since. It has made our relationship difficult due to financial restrictions and the uncertainty of the future."

"I should say the strains recession puts on relationships are very underestimated. The last two years have been awful. First my youngest son unemployed, then my husband, and both together at one stage. They are both now only partly employed."

"It helped to break up my first marriage."

The redundant partner may take "revenge" on the one who still successfully holds down a job by seeking consolation elsewhere:

"He was made redundant and started seeing a lot of my best friend. She had problems with her husband. She found out that he had been seeing someone else for two years. She was devastated and turned to us for sympathy and advice. While I was at work, they began going out together during the day and chatting – she about her problems and he about the difficulty of finding a new job. They eventually fell in love and had an affair. He told her he was going to leave me. She didn't want him to, because she thought too much of me and the kids and wanted to repair her own marriage. She also has a child. My husband told me about this in January. They are still seeing each other. I await his decision."

Two pensioners tell how the recession has affected their lives:

"Worsened it. Life is very restricted on the state pension only, plus a little deflated investment income, and he has become miserly and restrictive in every possible way, worried to death about how to meet commitments."

"After we retired, we purchased a lovely stone cottage and made a beautiful home and garden there. We built a stone and glass summerhouse and stone seats to sit on in the sun. It was enjoyable. But our son, 100 miles from us, had begun to feel the results of the recession and needed thousands to pay the Inland Revenue.

We sold up and moved south to be near him, his wife and three children and, as their debts piled up, our profit from the cottage sale diminished. His wife divorced him, their home was requisitioned, even the children's cycles were confiscated. Our son now lives with us, and his family is housed by the DHSS [now DHS] about 600 yards away. He works extremely hard when he can get the jobs, but some mornings he has to ask us for cash to buy petrol to get to work.

What the future holds for us all I don't know. We're in our 70s and don't want the hassle – we've both worked so hard all our lives."

Finally, three couples tell how they are weathering the storm:

"We have had it really tough. Defaulted on the mortgage, standing orders bounced, etc. Rising interest rates nearly finished us off. It has made us stronger and more united. If it's made our relationship stronger, that's the *only* thing the Tory party has ever done for us!"

"We have had a very tough three years and been through a lot of trauma. It hasn't changed our relationship, but we appreciate it more now. If we can survive this, we can survive anything."

"It hasn't affected us. We're quite broke but, as long as we're together, the simplest pleasures, like walking the dog, are a treat."

Hardship suffered jointly can make a couple even closer where their love is strong already, but when one partner is suddenly thrown into dependency on the other and the balance between them is upset, the relationship enters potentially very dangerous waters.

The answers to the previous question (and those on page 150) show that most women who give up work out of choice to become full-time mothers find it hard adjusting to financial dependency. It is obviously much more difficult if you get thrown out of your job. It is especially painful for a man, brought up in a competitive culture of male achieving and providing, to face the fact that he is "redundant" – a word with dreadful emotional connotations – and to come to terms with living off his partner's income. Sexual potency for men and for women is inextricably linked with self-respect, and self-respect for most people is linked to the ability to earn one's living. Men are less resilient than women because male culture seeks to deny the emotions, so failure (like illness and bad luck) hits them harder, because it brings a torrent of feelings of inadequacy they are not equipped to cope with.

The danger is that as depression creeps up on the unemployed husband, he will no longer see the marital home as a refuge but as a trap in which he is stuck, while his wife comes and goes to her job. He may start to resent her independence and her earning power, and to blame her for his predicament.

Reassurance from the wage-earning partner does not seem to help women who don't like being dependent on men, and coming from a woman to a man who feels wounded anyway, it could be taken as condescension. In a household where loss of income may be causing severe financial strain, emotional tension can reach breaking point.

The most important thing for the partner who is made redundant is to hang on to – or regain – self-respect. This means doing something worthwhile with your time, and grasping the opportunity to make a change. A crisis can open doors into a different future. Stand back from your immediate situation and take as wide an overview as you can. Try to break down your old unexamined assumptions and rethink what you really want from work and from life. Consider studying or training for a change in direction. Or get out of the rat race and take on a low-pressure job that puts you in contact with friendly people. Keep considering new options and keep an open mind.

Above all, keep talking to your partner, and if you start to feel resentful of him or her, don't bottle it up, but tell them so. It will do you good to talk out your feelings, and to work through this difficult time together. Although there are no easy solutions, pain is more bearable to both of you if it is shared.

How do you share responsibilities of home/childcare?
Are you satisfied with your present arrangements?

A British social attitudes survey conducted in 1993 showed that men spend half as much time as women on household duties. It also showed a considerable discrepancy between what men say and what they do: 75 per cent of men felt that they should share the washing-up equally, but only 35 per cent did so. Household chores that men were most likely to share were the washing-up, and after that the shopping, cleaning, cooking and laundry, in that order.

A factor that complicates equal sharing is that most women spend some months or years at home looking after young families. At this stage, couples who have been used to sharing housework often split their responsibilities and assume the traditional male and female roles. This can cause alienation, and resentment on the part of women who feel their lives have become no more than a round of domestic duties.

On the other hand, if a woman is at home all day, it is not reasonable that she should still expect her partner to do 50 per cent of the chores. The right balance is all the more difficult to achieve when men see themselves as "helping" with home and childcare, because this reinforces the traditional idea of domestic work as the woman's domain. It causes animosity in a relationship when a woman has to ask her partner to do the washing-up or sort out a quarrel between the children. She feels stress and resentment that she has to ask for her partner's involvement in his own home and family; he feels the same, because even if he doesn't find the chores demeaning, he doesn't like being told what to do.

Responsibilities for running the home are basic to any couple who live together, and are a source of friction in about two thirds of the relationships examined in this book. It is essential to discuss your attitudes towards home- and childcare in realistic detail before moving in together if you want to avoid hostility and resentment. If you work out a plan of collaboration that satisfies both of you, it will give your relationship a solid foundation.

The following contributors are satisfied with shared responsibility:

"We always have shared these responsibilities. I feel this has been a large part of the success of our relationship."

"We share the chores. He doesn't see it as 'helping' me. We both clear up the dirt we both make. He has been marvellous adapting to a teenage stepdaughter and has spent hours at a time helping me to recover from a bad relationship with her father and doing all the 'fatherly' things – school runs, homework, problems etc. I am indebted to him."

"Responsibilities for home and childcare have always been shared from day one. My husband saw our children born and was never bothered about changing nappies etc. Me, I can wallpaper and paint along with him."

"My husband is brilliant. When I was working full-time we shared everything. He cooked, cleaned, (better than I did, to be honest), and is more practical and domesticated than myself. He was excellent too when the children were young, more patient and better at playing with them than me."

"I gave up work to have our daughter and I insist that I do almost all the housework. He takes an active part in her care and upbringing and is not at all shy of dirty nappies and the like."

"I do most of the home/childcare. He does his share when he is here and will cooperate most of the time. I was at home with the children for 16 years – out of choice – so most of these responsibilities have been mine. Now I am working again we all have to pull our weight and I am mostly satisfied with the arrangement."

"When he was at home, we split the chores like this: he did shopping, cooking, cleaning kitchen, dishes, some hoovering, washing cars and checking them for oil, water etc., helped with bathing and dressing children, some repair jobs and house maintenance. I did washing, ironing, tidying, most of cleaning, looking after children and Nana, all paperwork and bills. We had outside help with cleaning and gardening."

Housework arrangements need to be flexible to accommodate the other activities of both of you. In retirement, chores can usually be shared more equally. One retired man describes an unusual arrangement that works well for him and his wife:

"We share the cooking and shopping two weeks on and two weeks off."

For women whose partners don't take on a fair share of domestic responsibility, it's a major source of dissatisfaction in their relationship:

"We don't share. Not satisfied."

"Not satisfied. My husband cooks and will babysit. I do the remainder but would like him to do more. I hardly go out so do more childcare than him. My mum looks after our son for us both to work full-time."

"He does only what is asked, nothing routinely. He cares for the children while I work evenings."

"I totally manage home and childcare. As I work part-time there is no alternative, but I sometimes wish my husband had more time to devote to both."

"I do it, then shout at him. I hardly ever get the cooperation, even if I ask, before or during housework. I'm very unhappy about this and wish he would automatically join in instead of being nagged."

"I see to the children and house. He just works."

For the next two, lack of male involvement was disastrous:

"My first husband realized the importance of sharing when it was too late."

"My ex wanted nothing to do with helping to run, clean and keep home, and he never helped with my daughter. We have been divorced 5½ years and he has not once seen her or been in contact or helped with financial provisions."

For the woman who finds it difficult combining a full-time job with all the housework, the solution is *not* to give up her job!

"This has been the subject of many arguments. Throughout the early years he worked long hours to provide for us. It seemed only natural for me to do everything else. Gardening, decorating, childcare, housework. Even when I had a full-time job. I did shopping at lunchtime etc. He said, if you can't manage, give up your job. It's not the actual work that I object to, but picking up after everyone. Our girls are 21 and 25 and do not want to leave. Dad pays for everything and mum does the housework."

The woman above has become a drudge to her husband and children. Both boys and girls should be brought up to clear up their own mess. It's particularly important for boys to clear up after themselves, so that they will grow up with a sense of domestic responsibility. The woman below is passing the mistakes of one generation on to the next, reinforcing her husband's attitude, and training her son to grow up just like him, thinking men are born to be waited on:

"The main problem is that my husband doesn't tidy up after himself and I get very angry about this. I don't mind tidying up after my son but I think my husband should tidy up after himself – I am not his maid!"

Unusually, this woman, married to a "know-it-all" whom she doesn't love, wants to keep the housework to herself:

"He always interferes in it. He thinks he always knows better because he's older than me."

The next couple have no children and are both at work.

"I do all the work. I have moaned about this, but he points out that when he does household chores, I criticize him for not doing them properly. I know this is true."

That comment shows that if you want to share responsibilities you have to agree on joint standards. Some men perform household chores deliberately sloppily, so that their wives will stop asking them. You need to agree priorities. Hygiene is most important in kitchens and bathrooms, but how much does dust matter elsewhere?

Two women comment on the double standard that says the man's job is more important than the woman's. Who stays home when the washing machine has to be fixed? (It's quite possibly not the person who knows most about machines, who would be better placed to make sure the mechanic isn't a cowboy.)

"My husband works long hours. The responsibilities of home/childcare are predominantly mine, also most of the finances. This arrangement is fair under current circumstances. However, I often wonder why it is that if I want to do anything (job or training) it is always down to me to make suitable arrangements for our children."

"What irks me is that when one of the children is ill it always falls on me to stay at home, even though we both work full-time. We've no extended family in the area to help."

The next woman, a 32-year-old in a high-powered managerial job, lives completely under her husband's double standard.

"He was made redundant two years ago. This really knocked his confidence and he has been depressed ever since. I am not at all happy with current arrangements. He is happy to allow me to do all shopping, cooking, cleaning etc. He rarely helps voluntarily and does it reluctantly if asked."

It sounds very much as though her husband is "getting his own back" on her for having lost his job. She says: "He wears his underwear too long and does not shower enough. He slops food on his clothes and picks his nose in front of me. He won't make love more than once in every four to six weeks." He is resentful of her position, and he uses laziness and slovenly behaviour as a way of "punishing" her for her success and his own failure and misfortune. It's possible that she puts up with what most women would find unacceptable because she feels guilty that she has what he wants: a good job. If she realized what was going on under the surface of their relationship, she might be able to help him to change, or to make some necessary changes herself.

Finally, here's a man who would like to break down the traditional roles, but whose wife is possessive about childcare:

"Wife housekeeps, I decorate and repair. She tends to take control over childcare – I would like to be more involved in this."

And here's one who has his head in the sand:

"I don't take any responsibility. Yes, I am happy."

 ## Q: What are your happiest times together?

For those in good relationships, simply being together is happiness:

"When all the family are together, playing and having fun. Doing simple things."

"When we can laugh at ourselves and share time with friends."

"Day out together as a family."

"We have always been happy just to be together. Now the children are off our hands we can spend more time together alone, which is lovely."

Even the drabbest chore can make you happy when you share it with the one you love:

"Doing things together, e.g. cleaning the car . . ."

Many cited their high points as giving birth, making love and other shared intimacies:

"When our children were born we felt very close."

"Giving birth, on holiday, in bed."

"When we are in bed together, just sitting together, out together . . ."

"In the evening alone, listening to music, reading, massaging his feet."

"Holidays. Making love. Family projects, e.g. painting the house."

"Usually when we are watching the twins and finding it incredible that we produced two such wonderful beings. Being out all together in the sun. Doing simple things."

Family activities and projects came high on the list of pleasures:

"When we're hiking, camping, picnicking, doing things together, sharing new experiences. When we talk and listen to each other."

"When we are all together as a family. Relaxing in the garden. Out with friends. Christmas is especially happy."

"There have been so many good times. Wonderful memories of holidays with family and friends. Just laughing together at something silly!"

"Must include planning and getting the two houses we've lived in."

Older contributors often mentioned the companionship of animals:

"Walks. In the garden with the dogs and cats."

"Walking the dogs. Sitting together peacefully, having a cuddle. Laughing."

It's interesting to note that all are simple pleasures and most are free. Not having money causes a great deal of worry, but inner happiness does not depend on it.

Q. What are your worst times together?

For a few, there are no worst times together: the worst times are when they are apart:

"When we are apart or one of us is working very hard and we can't get time together as a family."

For the majority, the worst times are when they are together without the sense of togetherness. Most couples rate arguing as their unhappiest activity.

"Arguing over what to spend and what not to spend; saving electricity, water, petrol; washing up (he does it under the tap); never going out together; going on self-catering holidays – he wants to lie on the beach, I want to explore."

"When we try to shop together, there is always an argument."

"Arguing or sulking."

"When we argue over money etc."

"When I have PMT I can be very unpleasant and ruin everything."

"Queuing anywhere. He is impatient."

Arguing need not always be destructive. It is much better to release anger when you feel it than to bottle it up, because a delayed explosion will probably be much bigger than is warranted by the situation that triggers it. Anger suppressed indefinitely is now believed by researchers into cancer to be one of the prime causes of serious illness. Unacknowledged anger is also often at the root of deep depression.

The main fear in releasing anger is that it will cause rejection. Often, parents who can't handle their children's anger either ignore it or laugh at it, and when a child is angry about something important to her, this belittling behaviour can be very hurtful indeed – a lesson in denying or suppressing her emotions. As the pattern is repeated, the child grows up believing that anger will be followed by rejection.

In any adult partnership, there comes a point when strength of feeling will be tested by anger. It gives a great sense of security to discover that your relationship can contain your anger and that your partner's love does survive it.

There are, nevertheless, positive and negative types of argument. Protracted bickering, the reopening of old wounds, pointless abuse, and rows that veer wide of the mark, particularly those fuelled by alcohol, are likely to leave you just as far apart as when you started, but exhausted.

If, on the other hand, you argue constructively, speaking with the passion you feel to get your message across as clearly as possible, listening closely, questioning your partner to make sure you understand the other point of view, and always looking for common ground on which to build, your argument can reach a positive conclusion that will bring you closer together.

Arguing positively can be exhilarating. Anger is, after all, another form of passion, and if you feel passionately about your partner, then he or she is bound to make you passionately angry from time to time.

For some women, the problem is not arguing, but their partner's refusal to discuss important issues.

"When there are problems that he won't discuss and I want to clear the air."

The next woman managed to save her marriage by getting her husband to talk about the difficult feelings he was suppressing:

"We have had some sticky patches because of the pressure of my husband's work. He is a police officer and did six months with the child protection team, when he was dealing – sadly – with abused children almost the same age as our daughter. The hours were incredibly long and I was spending most evenings by myself. When he was home he was very snappy and wound up. It was a very difficult time. I'd had enough after a while and told my husband either he changed, or left the team, or left me. I think he was quite shocked by this, and although I'd told him often before how I felt, it really sank in this time. He started saying how bad he felt having to interview the children etc., and once he started to talk to me again, we were fine. At the time I didn't feel I liked him very much, though love was still there under the surface."

But the following woman has given up trying, and her marriage is disintegrating:

"When we start discussing the state of our relationship – I don't bother now."

Some couples feel least together when pressures from outside intrude on them. In-laws and children cause most disruption:

"When the in-laws are around. When we are desperate for money and the bills start pouring in."

"When his mother visits at Christmas. She dislikes me and vice versa so it's very strained and I try not to see her for the rest of the year."

"When there's not enough time to spend on ourselves and there are a lot of pressures from outside. When the kids are having their normal teenage rebellion and try to play one of us off against the other."

"Nightimes, when children disturb sleep."

Babies and young children are inevitably going to give you sleepless nights, and if you're tired and exhausted you will feel ratty and fractious with one another. Some men believe that they shouldn't have to get up in the night for children if their partners are at home all day. This attitude causes resentment, as it puts women on family duty all round the clock. Flexibility is the only solution. Share beds, swap beds, take shifts if necessary to get as much rest as you can. As long as you support each other and realize that the problem is temporary, you will be able to surmount it.

A united front is also vital on matters of child discipline, or children will cause mischief between you, as testing out their own power is part of growing up.

You need to work out a joint policy on in-laws too, especially if they are interfering and possessive of their son or daughter. Visits at their house, rather than yours, can be ended when you wish to end them, and, of course, only one of you need go. In-laws who like to be involved can be very helpful, taking your children off your hands so that you have more time together alone.

For some people in poor marriages, togetherness is itself unhappy:

"Evenings, when he is tired and preoccupied with work. He doesn't like TV and I don't like his classical music."

"Domesticity."

"Watching telly most nights."

"Being stuck in a traffic jam with the children. Wet weekends in the house."

"In the house, in the evening, with tired children around us, when he loses his temper."

"On holiday. We need space."

"Being in the house all day. Not being able to afford to go out. When he is drunk."

"When I am in a very talkative mood and maybe a bit scratchy he shuts off from me. He puts his nose in a book and doesn't answer me."

This woman's partner is unemployed and suffering severe depression:

"If I've been out working and I come back and he's still in bed, I hate it."

Some mention specific sexual and emotional problems that have pushed them apart:

"In bed when he wants sex and I don't."

"When I feel I can't be myself when we are making love."

"When we discussed liaisons with others."

"When I found out he had had an affair with my best friend. When I was having alcohol problems."

"Last year I was suffering from depression and this put a great strain on the relationship. However, following my illness we have become a lot closer emotionally and physically and been better able to cope with family life."

Others have survived disasters together:

"The worst time was in 1980 when my husband had a near-fatal car crash. The last couple of years of recession have been a real test of the strength of our marriage."

"Few. Both having to work day and night at one point to save for a house – which made us very tired. Bad car crash. The realization that we are likely to remain childless."

"Following the death of my second daughter (stillborn)."

"When our youngest son was killed in a road accident."

 What is the worst row you have ever had?

Some people can't remember now what their worst row was all about. Lapse of memory may be due to drink, or to the triviality of the argument itself:

"I don't remember the cause but we had been married about three years and our daughter was a few months old. We rowed and my husband packed a bag and walked out. The car wouldn't start and he had to come back. The suitcase had half my clothes in it. We collapsed laughing."

A few say their worst row was about money — one man lost a lot of money gambling. More common are rows about childrearing and discipline (see also page 183), such as those that occur in the following household:

"About our daughter's lifestyle. My husband doesn't like it and nor do I, but I try to keep out of things and hope they will sort themselves out, whereas he tries to lead her life for her."

But around three quarters of those who answered this question say that their worst ever rows have been about sexual jealousy.

"About his ex-girlfriend. Friends told me how cut up he was when their relationship ended and his family mentioned her at every opportunity. I told him to go back to her or tell them to shut up. It worked – now they ignore me. But I married him, not his relatives!"

"Having not seen him for 6 months we went to a ball and he danced with my friend and not me, then walked home with her, while I was left to bring up the rear with her husband, who was drunk. Boy, was that a row."

"When I found out that he had been seeing my friend again after I thought it had all finished."

"A few weeks ago I flew at him because he wouldn't make love to me. I said it was because he loved B [her best friend with whom he is having an affair], and why didn't he love me any more? I hit him and hit him."

"Two years ago, after he was informed of the affair I had had (by my lover's girlfriend)."

"He is extremely jealous of me, but expects me to understand his liking for a lady friend of his. This creates problems that lead to pretty bad rows."

"It was caused by me, doubting his faithfulness. We shouted – he hit me – and we had quite a bad few months thereafter with similar rows and plate-throwing."

"It was deemed that I was ignoring her presence, i.e. focussing my attention on the other young women present. It was a misunderstanding of intent."

"I knew I was winding him up but I had to push him to test him almost – it was over my jealousy after he had had drinks and gone out with his ex-wife."

"Mainly about jealousy. When he found out about my affair he was furious with me and very frightening. I thought he would kill me – I think he could have done."

"He accused me of being unfaithful and walked out. I took an overdose."

"When I confronted my husband with his feelings about a girlfriend of ours. I was shaken to the core when he said he loved her and had asked her to live with him!"

"When my partner went to a party with a girlfriend before we were married and stayed out all night. It created a real feeling of mistrust."

When asked later on in this survey to name the most important single ingredient for a good relationship, more people voted for *trust* than any other quality, including *love*. One woman puts it this strongly: "Without trust, you're dead."

What singles out marriage from any other sexual partnership is the pledge of exclusivity. As one woman puts it: "Fidelity is the one thing, at the end of the day, that makes a relationship special, unique to you two alone." Exchanging vows of fidelity makes you strong in unity; extremely vulnerable in doubt. Another woman writes: "If you trust someone completely, respect them too, you will get the maximum love/satisfaction over the years. You will also get hurt the most if/when you discover they have lied to you." She found out that her husband, whom she believed to be faithful and with whom she thought she had a good, close, sexually fulfilling relationship, had been having one-night stands for 12 years.

The discovery – or even the suspicion – of infidelity destroys trust, and therefore eats away at the core of the relationship.

Other, non-sexual, types of jealousy can also be pernicious if you fear your partner does not put you first.

"I was jealous of his children and he realized that I was trying to manipulate it so they wouldn't be around."

"When he came home late without ringing and I accused him of preferring his pub cronies to his family. When he was not happy in a temporary job – this caused frustration on both sides."

"Recently when I had a disagreement with his sister, who is a lot older than him. He refused to support me because he is unable to stand up to her."

"It was when we were newly married and living with my mother and her new husband. I can remember being on my knees and begging them to understand (I can't remember what) and help me, and they were stony-faced and embarrassed because I was creating a scene and my husband was cowering in the kitchen instead of defending me. We rowed about it later and I was so angry and upset that I literally threw our baby son at him and stormed out of the house. I was gone for several hours, but he didn't come looking for me. When I got back he said he had been worried about me but there was no apology for not standing up for me, and I learned that no one was going to stand up for me but me – and I wasn't strong enough then."

Even if her husband didn't agree with her point of view, he should have had the strength to protect her – as any good friend and ally of either sex would have done – if only against humiliating herself. A caring partner can take control when things are getting out of hand, and bring some dignity and common sense to an embarrassing situation. He could have put his arm round her and led her away to talk over the problem, rather than cowering in the kitchen.

A further group of people had their worst arguments not about sexual jealousy, or about other types of jealousy, but about sex itself. Again, at the core of the argument, was a feeling of not being put first. This next woman complains that her husband shuts her out of his private thoughts:

"All our arguments are about sex – the fact that I want it more often. But the worst row we had was when I felt my husband was not sharing all his innermost thoughts. This, to me, is truly a bond between a couple. He admits he doesn't like to argue back in a quarrel because he is 'frightened' of upsetting me. Therefore, he is quiet, then I think he doesn't care, and bingo! A row."

The 77-year-old woman who has been frustrated by her husband's impotence for 45 years was crushed by his preference for pornography.

"I found his collection of porno magazines 40 years ago and threatened to leave him. If he refused to do it, why read about it? – Why waste money? They certainly never *helped* him."

Thankfully couples today can seek help and avoid the terrible humiliation that this woman and her husband must have suffered.

 What is the usual pattern of your arguments and how do they end?

Some manage successfully to talk things through without losing their tempers:

"We don't argue nowadays. We talk and then compromise if we still disagree."

"We have never had a row, only slight disagreements. If we have different points of view, we talk it over rationally, putting our different cases, and then reaching a compromise."

Then there are people in good relationships who need to let off steam at each other from time to time in a healthy row that clears the air and renews their closeness:

"Usually caused by financial worry. We argue. I slam doors and cry in temper. Invariably we end up laughing and never sleep or part without making up. Lovemaking usually follows."

"We both flare up very quickly and don't back down easily. We really shout, slam doors, throw the odd object, walk out – then within an hour we'll be apologising and making up."

"We have our say, make our points, then agree/agree to differ and forget about it. Neither of us is the type to keep dragging things up. We agreed very early on in our relationship to speak out about things before they became mountainous, and on the whole this has worked well. I feel we are both honest with each other, which is usually the best policy."

"Mad heated row, followed by huffing for one hour max, and then kiss and make up. We are never huffy long-term."

"We disagree about something, shout at each other, don't speak for a while, then kiss and make up and apologise."

"Shout – ignore – make up – cuddles – sex, sex, sex."

A larger number of contributors have arguments that are unconstructive: damaging and inconclusive. The trouble with having a row that doesn't end in the fresh air of understanding and reconciliation is that the unresolved bad feelings fester beneath the surface and will flare up in stale recrimination next time something triggers an argument. The poison circulating in the system gradually builds up and eats away at the good feelings you have for your partner until there's nothing left.

"We shout and don't manage to put our sides of it without hurting each other."

"Tears, recriminations, swearing, hitting, storming out."

"We don't argue much, but usually [the arguments] end with one saying 'Oh, shut up', and all going quiet."

"We don't argue very much. Usually a disagreement, not speaking for a day or two, then gradually returning to normal."

"My husband is too quick to order me about. He leans on me. I wish our arguments could be more constructive."

"He is unable to argue logically – he is slightly dyslexic. He rants and raves. I have schooled myself not to cry, over the years. There is no reconciliation or apology and I can't speak for days."

The majority of contributors identified the usual course of their arguments as follows: the woman names the subject that is causing disharmony; the man denies that a problem exists; the woman's behaviour becomes insistent and dramatic; the man refuses to participate and walks away. Here are some examples:

"I try to talk to him about how I feel. He ends up slamming the door and going to bed."

"My husband does not speak – sometimes for weeks on end. He always apologises – by letter."

"Usually over the same thing – his lady friend, whom he insists will not come between us. He goes off to bed."

"He accuses me of nagging. I complain of his untidiness. We end up coming out with more and more examples of what the other one does to annoy. In bad cases he storms out and will not speak for one to four days."

"He leaves the room or drives away."

"We argue very very rarely and if we do it usually ends up with him walking away and we don't speak for 24 hours or so."

"We don't have many – he says nothing and I finish up crying on my bed."

"I usually grumble about being stuck in a rut, and about him working extra hours for no extra money. It ends with him going quiet."

Why is this pattern so prevalent? Does it mean, according to the common male view, that women are "picky" – "nags" who "henpeck" their husbands? Are men superior, because they are above "petty" arguing?

These examples show men and women handling conflict in different ways. As carers, women's instincts tend towards creating harmony and understanding. This means that they are more likely to be aware of misunderstandings at an earlier stage than their male partners, who traditionally shut out and deny the world of emotions. Men quite genuinely may not recognize what is going wrong, because their emotional responses are less finely tuned.

But the male response: "I don't know what you're talking about: I can't see any problem", is exasperating to the woman, to whom the problem is by now only too clear. Frustrated, she explains again. If he still doesn't understand, she shouts, to try to get him to listen.

Men who are not at ease in the world of emotions anyway, find emotions that have got out of hand impossible to cope with. What they understand best is action, and they act to take control by removing themselves from the situation.

By remaining silent and refusing to participate, or physically walking out, a man asserts his dominance and appears to "win" the argument. Remember that *winning* is more important in the competitive male culture than reaching common understanding, which is the female objective. So he "wins", and his partner is defeated – frustrated, at her wits' end, crying or howling unheard.

But the real loser is the relationship. Relationships exist because people communicate with each other. If one party blocks communication as a means of asserting superiority, the connection is lost and the balance is lost. The one who is cut off will feel insecure and disorientated. Frustration and rage will naturally result. Men who blame women for losing their tempers should understand their own part in this mechanism.

Men want and expect their partners to love and care for them. This cannot happen without interaction. Men need to take responsibility for their side of the relationship, and this means listening, being involved, giving an opinion, admitting vulnerability, and sorting things out together. A man who shuts off or walks away is rejecting his partner. This is how women fall out of love with men, it's how relationships break down, and it explains why many more divorces are instigated by women than by their husbands.

 Has there ever been any physical violence between you? If so, what happened?

The puzzling thing about the answers to this question was that so few women admitted to having been beaten (see pages 90–93). According to one survey, one in ten women has suffered marital rape, and a probation service report indicates that domestic violence accounts for nearly

50 per cent of all violent crime, but police are often reluctant to inter-vene, and much wife-battering goes unreported. Women are often blamed for being victims – for "asking for it" - and therefore they are ashamed of confessing. It could be that most battered wives who saw the questionnaire were unable to fill it in. Yet acknowledging that there is a problem is the first step towards putting it right.

When passions are running high, the urge to lash out sometimes becomes uncontrollable. In the examples that follow, it's usually the women who crack under the strain. It's evident by the way they write that no real damage is done: their marriages are strong enough to encompass the occasional tantrum.

"Several occasions. Only me. I hit him and throw things. I'm getting better. I only go for the cheap vases now and I throw them against the wall."

"Only by me perhaps hitting out at him, and then only really in frustration, not meaning to hurt him. He has never hit me. He hits doors etc. instead."

"I hit out very occasionally and instantly regret it. My husband is very against violence of any kind and I try to stop myself."

"I did once lash out at him in a frenzy, and he hit me back. It did the trick."

"Once. He hit me – bang! I can't remember what we were arguing about but I do remember I deserved it."

In some cases, self-control is precarious because of other factors, and violence is easily triggered:

"No. I've thrown things when suffering from PMT, but not since I was put on the Pill to control my periods."

"Yes, I hit her on more than one occasion on account of my nervous breakdown."

According to a survey of 500 patients of general practitioners in England, premenstrual tension (PMT), or premenstrual syndrome (PMS), as it is also called, affects 75 per cent of women in varying ways. A woman who is usually happy and positive may suffer a dramatic character change towards the onset of her period because of depression, tiredness and irritability. She may become morose, bitter, violent towards herself and others, and is 30 times more likely to commit a crime such as shop-lifting. There is an urge to drink alcohol, but at the same time, the body is less able to process it. A woman suffering from PMS gets more drunk more quickly, and is likely to be aggressive. Symptoms tend to increase in severity from the age of about 36 to the menopause.

The symptoms of PMS are likely to make life unpleasant for all those closest to the sufferer; her husband or partner in particular, often has to bear the brunt of her mood swings. Premenstrual irritability is more common in married women than in those living alone, and may bring the man who has to put up with it to the brink of despair. One gynaecologist has suggested that PMS could be a major cause of marital breakdown, though some sufferers feel that marriage causes PMS!

Women who have no physical symptoms of PMS, such as cramps, backache or fluid retention, may be unaware that their violent outbursts could be driven by hormones. If you catch yourself behaving in a way that's frighteningly or depressingly out of character, check your diary, and keep a record to see if a pattern emerges.

PMS can be treated, and you need no longer make others suffer or be the victim of your own bad behaviour. See your doctor, and ask about hormone therapy, or you may prefer to consult a homoeopath or herbalist. Some women find that vitamin B6 helps. Two 50 mg tablets should be taken daily, from about three days before you would expect the symptoms to start, to about three days after you begin to bleed.

Violent rages are often alcohol-related:

"During a drunken rage years ago he set fire to his shirt and threw it at me."

"Many years ago we used to end up fighting after we had been out drinking, but we were both still in our late teens, so I put it down to that."

Some men lose their temper and hit out just once in their lives, then suffer the most bitter remorse:

"I got upset/hysterical the day we were burgled and was blabbering a bit. A whack round the face brought me back and then he was just so upset at having done it, and felt far too bad about it."

"Once on our first Christmas together. He had been drinking whisky and we had a tiff and he slapped me across the face. He was so upset afterwards that he cried and he stopped drinking spirits from then on."

Violence erupts most commonly in arguments about jealousy. This is not surprising, since most people have their worst ever rows over real or suspected unfaithfulness (see page 82).

"There was violence when I tried to leave him after his affair. He locked the door and wouldn't let me out. I broke a window with my fist to attract attention from a neighbour. The police came."

"Only once, when we were in bed together and I found out he had been seeing my friend when I thought it was all over. I hit him until I realized what I was doing and then I just cried bitterly."

"Yes, since he has been having an affair with my best friend. Usually when I try to hit him, he restrains me. He has never ever hit me back, but his evasive actions can hurt me."

"He says I'd have to cheat on him to see violence, and then he'd kill me!"

Violence in pregnancy

A different sort of jealousy can cause some men to become violent to their pregnant wives. This is a particularly despicable and shocking form of violence. If a man punches his pregnant partner on her belly, he is probably expressing resentment at her closeness to the unborn infant – a closeness that he feels excludes him, pushing him out from the number one place in her affections. Not surprisingly, the partners of the women in the next group of contributors have not proved to be good fathers.

"Yes, he once kicked me in the tummy while I was pregnant. More recently he punched me and bruised my arms."

"He threw a big roll of chicken wire at me and hit me when I was pregnant."

"He pushes me around. Gave me a black eye. Was violent when I was pregnant."

A woman who is hit or knocked on her belly will almost certainly be reassured by her doctor that no physical harm has come to her baby. The baby is well cushioned inside the womb in the bag of fluid in which he bobs about like a cork. Nevertheless, such violence does give serious cause for alarm. If your partner is jealous of a foetus, how much more jealous will he be of a baby whom he can see you feeding and taking care of? You should be very concerned for the wellbeing and safety of your baby, and it is vital that you don't keep your fears to yourself. Talk to a sympathetic health worker, such as your ante-natal teacher; at the very least, confide in a friend. You need advice and support, because in the long run you may be better off leaving your partner than running the risk of having him harm you or your child.

Victims of serious violence

Once a man has given way to the urge to batter his wife, the violence becomes addictive. Batterers are capable of enormous self-delusion, which allows them to continue to crush wives they claim to love.

"He has hit me maybe three or four times. He can't retaliate with words like I can. I hit out a few times earlier in our marriage, but I stopped, because he would hit back much harder."

"Yes, twice he's knocked me out."

"Yes. He hits me, pushes me. I was in hospital because of a head injury he gave me."

"I am returning your form as I am unable to help with your research. I am 63 years of age and married to a wife-beater (even now). I would find it very difficult to talk about this on paper."

The last woman gave her full name, address and telephone number. It was a call for help. Yet any letter written back to her could have been intercepted by her violent husband with devastating consequences.

No one should have to suffer the pain and humiliation women like her endure. She must seek help, but without the danger of alerting her husband to what she is doing, or the call for help will become one more revolution in the vicious circle that brings further violence upon her.

A beaten wife is a woman who has been forced to relinquish all control over her own life into the hands of a brutal husband. Because of "love" and "loyalty", she is often prepared to withstand repeated batterings, in the hope that her husband will reform. Or she may be financially trapped, as well as a prey to emotional blackmail. To get out of this situation, she must make, to start with, just one decision, to do something on her own and for herself that is totally outside his sphere of authority. And that is to find out the number of a telephone helpline in her area, to call it, and to keep the call a secret from her husband. To find a helpline number, look in your local phone book or phone your local Citizen's Advice Bureau, which you will find listed in Yellow Pages. This will be just the first move towards taking back responsibility for your own life. Help is available to those who are ready to help themselves.

According to one survey, 40 per cent of men have used violence in rows with their wives or partners, so if you ring one of these helplines, you know you won't be alone.

 Does being in this relationship mean a loss of individuality? If so, how and why?

In marriages where there is over-dependence, rather than interdependence, the sense of responsibility and having to consider the other person's wishes all the time can be claustrophobic.

"Yes, I miss freedom because of responsibility to my wife and family."

"Always being invited out as a couple. Having to consider the other person before doing anything."

"Yes. You become very dependent on the other person. You cannot often act without consulting them. Sometimes I do because I am quite a strong character. But then so is he."

One woman says giving up private pursuits is a small price to pay for togetherness:

"In a way, yes, I guess I don't do my own thing so much any more, but I prefer having someone to consider to being on my own. I don't think I've lost the real me at all."

Other women feel that their individuality has been submerged under motherhood (see also page 150) or under the thumb of a domineering and possessive husband.

"Yes, because I'm a mother and a wife. Before, I was a staff nurse who loved her job, freedom, spare time and life."

"Yes. As a mother you are no longer a separate person. People are just interested in your child."

"Yes. Though I do the accounts, my husband has total control over the finances. I find it very difficult to ask for money for clothes or for the children. I would like to make more decisions."

"Yes. He thinks of me as his property and has told me so on repeated occasions. He says he is the boss."

Several contributors with husbands in the Forces feel, like the following woman, that on marrying they became a mere adjunct to their husbands, almost ceasing to exist in their own right at all:

"Yes, I feel I'm 'his wife'. This is worse in the Forces where you are always referred to as 'so-and-so's wife'. I feel overshadowed by his job, and the importance of it, and I feel that he needed intelligence to succeed in his career, whereas my being a wife and mother needs none."

Paradoxically, a marriage that suffocates your individuality is difficult to get out of, precisely because it saps your strength and self-confidence. Two women who have managed to leave describe how being free again is allowing them to rediscover themselves.

"I totally lost my individuality right from the beginning. I have had counselling since, which has helped. I allowed him to walk all over me. I hope I can be strong in a future relationship."

"Yes, we parted six months ago. I am now finding myself and opening up and realizing new potential."

In the next marriage, it's the wife's laziness that is letting her slump into the role of wife and mother and lose her individual sparkle. Her husband recognizes the dangers of this more clearly than she does. He's probably aware that he will begin to lose interest in her unless she livens up.

"Yes, for me. Possibly lack of motivation on my part – not having the need to prove myself. He recognizes this and tries to encourage my other interests."

The contributors who are most fulfilled in their lives and their marriages are those who have kept a strong sense of their own individuality, and not allowed themselves to merge with the wallpaper. Knowing and being yourself is essential for personal happiness and, in a couple, for keeping love and sexuality alive.

"No, I fight hard to be me and not to change to fit in with some of his ideas. Although it can cause trouble sometimes, I think he likes that about me."

"No. We still do things on our own and always have. In fact, since being back at work I have felt more of an individual than before."

"We both still have our own friends, go out separately occasionally and do different things. It's important to be your own person."

"Not at all. Although neither of us feels complete without the other. We are like two halves that only make one whole when we are together, but we still retain our individuality. Our personalities are very different."

The next group of people describe how being in a relationship where you are fully known and accepted by your partner can be a liberating experience. Where two people love, support and encourage each other instead of trying to get each other to fit the mould, the relationship gives the individual enormous confidence and scope for growth and self-discovery. The greatest potential of a positive marriage must be that it offers both security and a centre from which both partners can go out into the world. Such a marriage will not lose its element of surprise.

"No. We let each other develop. It's fulfilling and releasing."

"No. We follow the advice of Khalil Ghibran: the oak and the cypress tree do not grow in each other's shadow."

"The opposite in fact. I know he loves me for what I am. Through his love I can be totally me. I feel more able to express my individuality."

"It could be so, but in fact, because of his support, I am more individual now than I ever was."

"No, quite the reverse. I feel I have grown and found more of myself. The relationship has opened my horizons, not narrowed them."

Q. Is your relationship the most important aspect of your life? If not, what is?

For a minority of married people, spiritual and personal development is their priority in life:

"It was not. Searching for inner peace was."

"No. To be happy in myself and to know where I'm heading in life is the most important for me."

"For both of us our faith in Jesus is first; we put each other second."

Others put their relationship on a par with personal achievement:

"No. I look at everything in context. Work and myself are also important in different ways."

"I would put my relationship on the same level as health and career, because without the success of one, all the others seem insignificant."

Many write that their relationship with their children is as important as that with their partners:

"It is one of the most important. So is my relationship with children, friends and other members of the family."

"It was, but now it is alongside being parents. The relationship between us and our relationship to the babies is of equal importance. They all go together."

Some put their children first and allow their partners to drop to second place:

"My son. I would lie for him, kill for him, die for him. He is my world and my husband has been relegated to second place."

"I have to be honest and say that my daughter takes priority at the moment. As she is only four I feel protective towards her – and feel my husband doesn't need that side of me. I am very aware, though, that one day she will be grown up and it will be just myself and my husband again, so I do make a great effort and [give] equal consideration to being a wife as well as being a mother."

The last woman recognizes the danger in relegating her partner to second place. Not only does this unbalance the relationship, opening up a space in her husband's life that he might one day need to fill by having an affair, it can also unbalance the child, who will know her mother puts her first. This gives the child an unreal sense of her own power that makes the family a less secure place for her to be in. It means she will be jealous when her parents are affectionate towards one another, because she feels her place as number one with her mother is being usurped. She could become resentful of her father and start clinging to her mother, which would alienate the man still further.

One woman has already reached the dangerous end of this process:

"Yes, my relationship is the most important aspect of my life at the moment, but I suspect my children have been until now, which may be at the root of our problems."

Her life continues to revolve around her daughters, even though they are now both grown up. Her husband lives and works abroad, and she spends alternate periods of three months with him, and then with her daughters back in the UK. Her husband has developed a serious relationship with another woman. Her comment above suggests she realizes only now that he must have been feeling she neglected him in favour of her daughters for years.

Other couples are wiser, realizing the value of putting each other first:

"Yes. We both work hard at keeping our relationship as good as it is. We don't take it or each other for granted. It means so much to us both that we will not jeopardize it."

"Absolutely the most important. I would not allow *anything* to cast a shadow between us."

"Yes. It wasn't for a while – my son was more important, but then my husband and I realized we'd still be together after he'd gone."

Finally, five disillusioned people, three men and two women, describe what happens when a marriage becomes "more a way of life than an important thing":

"My business. But I would like to have been able to say, my relationship."

"It was when we first married, but now staying in a job is."

"No. I'm more interested in gardening or reading a good book."

"No. Going out without him is."

"It became more a way of life than an important thing. We are separated now."

PREGNANCY

The discovery that you are pregnant by a partner you love is almost always a thrill, even if unplanned; it is also the beginning of a sometimes frightening journey into the unknown. The accounts here show signs of trouble ahead if the father-to-be isn't totally committed to parenthood; they also show how love can deepen if the baby is wanted. A baby can never cement a poor union, though it's likely to make a good relationship even stronger.

Q. Was this the right decision at the right time?

The answers to this question did not show a preference for starting a family at any particular age or point in a relationship. It seems most women feel that whenever they fall pregnant, whether it's planned or accidental, turns out to be the right time for them to start a family, because whatever doubts or reservations they have had (see page 101) then quickly fall away.

A resounding 95 per cent of the women questioned feel they made the right decision at the right time. On average, the age at which they first gave birth was 25, by which time they had spent about three years with their partners. The youngest first-time mother in this survey was 16; the oldest 39. The 39-year-old had been with her 62-year-old husband for 20 years before she gave birth, which was the longest time together before having a baby. She assumed they were infertile, so never took precautions. She describes getting pregnant as "a brilliant happening".

The 16-year-old went on to make a good marriage. She says:

"We both think it was the right time. We were going out together and both still at school. We became pregnant unintentionally, really, but we were very happy about it. We were very much in love, and married straight away."

One in 16 first babies was conceived accidentally, but in most cases, nonetheless welcome for that.

"Although my first pregnancy was unplanned, I was delighted to be pregnant. My husband was pretty shocked, but I think if we really hadn't wanted the pregnancy we would both have been more careful with contraception. I think waiting longer would have made it harder coping with the adjustments to family life."

"We met when I was 14 years old and he was 15. We started dating regularly when I was nearly 16, but we did not have sexual intercourse until over a year later, and four months after that I became pregnant. I was 17 and studying for my 'A' levels. He was 19 and working as a junior bank clerk. Our two families got together and arranged to marry us off. Our decision to start a family was, therefore, not planned.

Looking back, I would not recommend this as the best way to start married life, but for me personally, it's the best thing that ever happened to me. I have never once regretted what happened 26 years ago or anything about our life together since then."

Of the small percentage of women who feel they started their families at the wrong time, most wish they had waited longer before getting pregnant.

"We wanted to start a family as soon as we were married. I got pregnant after 12 weeks of marriage at age 23. Looking back, this was not the right decision."

The most common reason for regret was being too young and immature, and not having spent enough time together as a couple to really get to know each other, or to establish a secure home into which to bring children.

"It was too soon. We were young, idealistic and still discovering each other and developing our personalities."

"I felt very immature at 19 and we had no money or security."

A few felt that they had been pressured into parenthood by the expectations of other people.

"I wasn't quite ready. I felt pressured by my parents and my husband. We are practising Catholics."

"On one level it felt right — it was the 'right' thing to do as far as social conditioning and my biological clock were concerned. On a deeper, at that time unidentifiable level, it didn't feel right at all."

Q. What were your reservations about having children?

Up until the 1960s it was relatively unusual for a couple to remain childless out of choice. Since then, the Pill and wider opportunities for women in the world of work have meant that a woman in a relationship has far more freedom and control over her own destiny. Having children is no longer an automatic priority. Increasing numbers of women are putting off their first baby until their late 30s or early 40s, when their careers are well established, and although all the women who answered this question had gone on to have children, only 16 of them had done so without any reservations clouding their minds for at least a short while.

The following is a most unusually confident answer:

"No reservations. During our engagement we talked about having a family, and in fact even agreed on four sets of names (two of which we used)."

Quite a number worried about the effects of losing their income, and wondered whether they could afford to look after themselves and a baby with only one salary coming in.

Another very common fear was that the time-consuming responsibility of having a child would disrupt a happy marriage. Would the couple still have enough time and energy to devote to one another? Would it change and alienate them?

"I feared losing myself, losing my partner's respect, flopping into the mother role with no space for myself."

"How would I cope? How would it affect our relationship? Would I be a good parent?"

Some women expressed a fear of the unknown: they were wary of the strangeness of pregnancy and the pain of childbirth; one remembers worrying that her baby might be born handicapped; one worried that she might not love her baby when she saw him.

One woman felt a deep-seated though irrational fear that her baby might suffer in childhood as she had:

"I had had a very bad childhood. I was neglected and physically abused and grew up totally lacking in self-esteem. I felt deep down all childhood was like that and didn't want my children to suffer as I had."

101

A few looked beyond their immediate circumstances and were apprehensive on a wider scale.

"Worried about the state of the world, i.e. unemployment, future prospects for our baby, the environment and its problems."

And one longer reply shows the benefits of talking through all your reservations:

"We discussed what we thought would be the changes in our lifestyle: no sleep, lack of social life, financial problems. We felt we had got it all sorted out. In fact, once the baby had arrived, we found we didn't want to go out, we wanted to spend time with the baby. We discussed how we felt we might both focus on the baby and ignore each other. We decided not to do it, but once the baby arrived, found ourselves doing it nonetheless! Then we decided that we must set aside time daily for ourselves only. This time (whether it was 10 minutes or an hour) was devoted to us, not the baby.

My biggest reservation about having children was what kind of world these children would be raised in. So much violence, drugs – AIDS was just beginning to be talked about, and I realized that this child's life would be very different to my own. It would need far more educating about drugs, sex etc. than I ever needed. Sex can be fatal these days – something that my partner and I didn't have to worry about when we met. I was afraid that I might not be able to protect my child/teenager from the world outside."

More serious doubts

Major doubts that often led to problems later did emerge at this early stage. Sometimes couples find it very difficult to agree on whether to start a family or remain childless. This can cause a terrible dilemma. Which way do you move? A decision in either direction that's not wholehearted could endanger the future of the relationship.

Some women who went ahead and got pregnant were still worried whether their partners would take to fatherhood.

"My reservations were how my husband would react to being main wage earner and being a father."

One woman cites her husband's immaturity, another his fear of responsibility and of losing independence and freedom. Another woman says she was worried because her husband didn't even like children.

Looking further into the survey, it is possible to say with some conviction that both partners should want children equally, or their arrival will inevitably upset the marriage.

One woman, whose husband was a borderline case, sensed the risk she was running as she gently steered him towards accepting parenthood:

"No reservations for myself, only a little anxious about how it would affect my husband. I had an overwhelming yearning to have children. My husband was frightened at the prospect. So I felt I nudged (rather than pushed) him into it."

Two women in the survey admitted to not being cut out for motherhood:

"I was not a maternal person and perhaps would not have had children if he had not wanted them."

"I never had any maternal feelings, and this worried me. I thought they would come, but they didn't."

It would be only too easy to criticize couples who embark on parenthood without being wholly committed to it. Sometimes the pressure to have children is so strong that it takes over, becoming the driving force in the relationship and putting it at risk.

But if you want the relationship to last, it's important to put it first. Talk to each other about your reservations and find out whether you are really suited to parenthood, or whether you have always just assumed that having children was inevitable, because your parents and society in general expect it of you. Even if all your friends are becoming parents, it's important to choose your own path for yourselves, and above all to remember that you do have a choice.

 What made you want to start a family when you did?

There were many simple and satisfying answers to this question. A lot of women spoke of their desire for children to make their life complete, their deep longing to have a baby with the man they loved.

"A child felt right. The perfect result of our love for one another."

"We loved each other. Nothing else mattered."

"I loved my husband very much. Something told me it was meant to be."

Age was a deciding factor with many parents, though – oddly – it was given as a reason for not waiting any longer whether the woman was in her twenties or thirties. Women with much older husbands generally wanted to start a family in the early years of their marriage. Several thought like this:

"We both wanted children and wanted them young so that we could be close to them."

"My mother was 29 when she had me and always seemed very old compared with other children's mothers. I didn't want my children to feel the same about me."

Some felt the time was right because their relationship was well established and they had a secure nest for their children.

"We felt we had had enough time to get to know one another and get used to sharing our lives."

"We felt mature and secure, financially and emotionally."

Others were influenced in their timing by their family and friends.

"Age, and other friends of similar age having their first child."

"It was what we both wanted at the time, though I think also a little bit of it was what everybody was waiting to hear."

But whereas some wanted to become parents because everybody else was doing it, because their family expected it and it was "the right thing to do", others embarked on parenthood out of a sense of boredom or failure – because it was "*something* to do".

"I was in a rather boring office job that I did not particularly like and I couldn't wait to get pregnant. It was a sense of achievement and a way out of work."

"I had failed my exams twice and there was a possibility that I might fail a third time, so having a child seemed the right move."

104

"I was getting nowhere at work and I wanted to leave."

"Nothing else to do. We started a family as I couldn't get any work. My mother was always ill (cancer), and as the eldest female I had all the housework, cooking, all the shopping etc. to do from the age of 11 or 12 years. So looking after my own home was easy after looking after a family of six."

It is perhaps easier to understand the instinct of this last young woman to continue looking after a family of her own in a home of her own, than to appreciate the reasoning of the much more experienced older woman who wrote:

"Lack of direction in life – we'd 'done it all' – heading towards being too old to childbear."

Boredom with the world and all it has to offer seems a strangely negative reason to throw yourselves into a physically and emotionally demanding lifelong commitment, but perhaps "boredom" is another word for the emptiness and aimlessness sometimes experienced by childless couples who are seeking a purpose in life. The question has to be asked: Is it fair on the child to make him your purpose in life? Isn't it expecting too much of him, even before he's been born?

In two cases, it appears that the marriage was made – at least in the mind of one partner – solely for the purpose of having children. In each, a baby was conceived under a threat of the relationship ending. One man wrote of his:

". . . wife's threats to leave if we did not start a family. In fact she seemed more keen on leaving work than on starting a family."

And one woman said:

"My husband demanded that we had a child, or he said there was no point in staying married."

Another piece of manipulation was carried out by a young woman who later regretted it bitterly:

"I was 17 and pregnant when we got married. I wanted to get married and thought being pregnant would tie my husband to me. But when I found out I was pregnant I felt despair and realized that I couldn't cope with the responsibility."

In some cases, couples were motivated to start a family by a feeling of mortality. One woman had lost both her parents quite suddenly, and another wrote:

"My brother was ill with cancer. It somehow put things into perspective."

This need to restore life and love where it had cruelly been wrenched away was shared by a couple who had both suffered physical and mental abuse in their own childhoods:

"We both had horrendous childhoods, and wanted to give our child the upbringing we never had."

And finally, the following man writes, possibly with a slight touch of superciliousness:

"As Catholics we should increase and multiply like sand on the seashore."

The answers to this question show that there are many reasons for starting a family other than the simple desire to bring a baby into the world.

 Q. Were you worried that you would lose independence on having a child?

Because of financial pressures, some women have no choice but to return to work; for others in low-paid jobs the cost of childcare is prohibitive. The "benefit trap", where a single mother can't afford to stay at home on state security and can't afford a childminder if she works, led in one much publicized case in 1993 to a young mother leaving her toddler at home unattended all day.

About a third of the women in this survey who could afford to make the choice to stay at home were concerned about becoming dependent on their partners (see also page 65). Many found the thought of having to rely on them for money uncomfortable and humiliating.

"I have always been financially independent. I was not happy at the prospect of having to ask for every penny I needed to spend."

"Yes, I am fiercely independent and I have never relied on a partner before."

"I was worried as we had always shared finances and my husband does not handle emotional problems well."

One woman who had suffered a miscarriage found her husband's financial support difficult to accept, and his emotional support not quite adequate. She paints a sad picture of herself at this vulnerable time while she was waiting to conceive another baby.

"I lost my first child at four months and was devastated. I was in the Wrens at the time, spending part of the week on my base. I made the decision to leave, so that at least if I had a second miscarriage I would be with my husband, though I felt emotionally that he didn't really understand how much it had affected me. At least he would be there in body if not in mind.

We made the decision to keep separate bank accounts and my husband would pay in a set amount each month for housekeeping. I do find it hard having to ask if I want a new dress etc. – after all, he doesn't ask himself if he wants a new pair of trousers. I didn't like being financially dependent on him and still don't."

By contrast, another woman explains how she envisaged being a mother as a liberating experience.

"I feel that one does not lose independence when a baby comes along. In some ways a mother has more freedom, especially if she does not go out to work, as she is not tied to catching a certain train in the morning, she can have a break as and when she feels like it, she is not tied to a lunch hour to suit bosses etc. Financially and emotionally we trusted in God to supply our needs."

Some women who said that they were not worried about losing independence before they had children, realized once they were at home and looking after a young family that they had not thought through this issue carefully enough (see page 150). It needs to be discussed fully, because resentment can easily arise if the woman gives up a job that means not only earning power, but self-respect, stimulation, challenge and friendship with colleagues, to find herself on 24-hour duty as a wife and mother. Having a job can satisfy many needs in life, as borne out by this woman:

"I had been [a housewife and] financially dependent since marriage. The days seemed long and sometimes empty."

Until employers provide adequate creche facilities, women almost inevitably have to give up work for a time after their baby's birth. Though many women look forward to doing this, and choose not to return to work until their children are at school, a lot do find it difficult to adjust to being financially dependent on their partners. This is a time when male and female can diverge so considerably into roles of earner on the one hand and carer on the other, that togetherness is put at risk.

A couple who wish to remain close need to work as a team. Home- and childcare needs to be shared in order to be enjoyed fully. A woman who is looking after children also needs time for herself, for her own interests and her own friends. A man who spends most of his time away from home also needs to be involved with his family. Part of the pleasure of planning your family can come through working out with your partner how responsibilities are going to be divided so you can each get as much as possible out of family life. The knowledge that you are a team gives a good feeling of security.

Q: Was your partner worried about the responsibility family life would bring?

At least half of the fathers-to-be were worried about the responsibility they were taking on. That in itself is not necessarily a bad thing, because it shows an awareness of the major change in lifestyle that a baby will bring. More disturbing were answers that reveal an inability to discuss the issue. Several women think their husbands were worried, but wouldn't admit it. One writes:

"He doesn't talk, so I didn't know he was worried until the reality hit some time after our son was born."

In other cases, unresolved anxieties affected the health of the fathers-to-be:

"Yes he was, despite his eagerness to have a child. He suffered a lot from migraines."

"Yes, in a word. He had palpitations and really worried about the extra responsibility of supporting us."

"Yes. This was one of several triggers that caused my husband to develop agoraphobia."

How much better it is to acknowledge your reservations about becoming parents beforehand, and talk them over openly until they are resolved one way or another, than to have the meaning of it all suddenly strike once the pregnancy is underway, like it did for this woman's husband:

"The responsibility of it all was felt by my husband when he felt the first kick of the baby and realized how much we were relying on him."

Such a discovery can cause a rift in a relationship at a very vulnerable stage. If women want their partners to be actively involved in sharing parenthood, it must be good sense to make sure they are ready for the responsibility, and looking forward to it, before going ahead. It puts a great strain on the relationship if the father is not fully committed to family life, and means most of the physical and emotional work of bringing up the child will fall on the mother.

 ## How did you imagine having a baby would change your relationship?

Strangely, some parents-to-be never gave this matter a moment's thought; others imagined that having a baby would not change their relationship. However, the most frequent answer to this question was a very positive one:

"I imagined it would draw us closer to care for another human being who belonged to us; whom we had created together."

People who thought positively about parenthood imagined that it would deepen and enrich their relationship and strengthen their love; looking after their baby would be a further dimension of life that they could share, and one that confirmed their commitment to the future. One woman says that she looked forward to discovering more about herself and her partner through parenthood, and another that it would make her union with her husband whole.

Yet there were a number of negative answers that signalled trouble ahead:

"I worried that my husband might feel pushed aside and be jealous and that we would not be free to do as we pleased."

"I was afraid we would have no time for each other and grow apart."

"My husband likes going to the pub, so I knew that there would be times when I would get fed up with staying in while he was out, but I really didn't imagine our relationship changing as much as it did."

"I sensed that we would disagree on basic issues of upbringing, because my husband and I were brought up so differently."

One woman had a successful, practical approach:

"Restrictions on social life and strain of broken nights might stress our relationship, but we talked it out a lot beforehand."

There is no doubt that the presence of a baby in the house can be very disruptive, at least until you establish a routine and manage to get enough sleep. You can minimize the disruption by agreeing on how you will deal with it together. The woman whose husband takes refuge from domestic difficulties in the pub is heading for trouble in the shape of a massive amount of responsibility landing on her shoulders.

The woman who fears her husband might be jealous should ask herself whether the prospect of having a baby makes her feel possessive or over-protective. Open up and allow your partner to feel that the baby is as much his as yours. Involve him as much as possible in every aspect of looking after the baby.

So much attention is paid to pregnant women that fathers-to-be sometimes feel left out. Read up about pregnancy and childbirth together, and if he can't visit ante-natal classes with you, at least share with him what you learn there. You can visit the hospital together to familiarize yourselves with the set-up in the delivery ward. Most couples nowadays feel it is very important for the father to be present at the birth. Men find it a powerfully emotional experience, and it creates a strong family bond from the start.

Keep the feeling alive that the baby belongs to both of you, and when she arrives, remember that you are not the only one who knows how to hold her and bath her. You are both absolute beginners. The excitement and adventure is in learning together how to handle your baby and in developing your bond as a family.

The woman who is worried about differing attitudes to bringing up children makes a very good point. It may seem ridiculous to consider your attitude to disciplining teenagers before you even get pregnant, but since discipline is the issue over which parents fight most, it will make your lives much easier if you present a united front from the start (see also page 183).

One or two people who answered this question expressed unrealistic hopes of what having a baby might do for their relationship. One woman imagined that it would make a cool relationship feel close and warm, and another who was insecure hoped that it would make her feel confident, loved and wanted.

Having a baby is not a solution to a problem and it is unlikely to cement a fragile bond. If a relationship has significant flaws, the arrival of a baby will most likely exacerbate them; if the relationship is strong and loving, a baby will probably make it more so.

Q: How did you imagine having a baby would change your personality?

One in five women either did not think motherhood would change their personalities at all, or never gave the matter a thought. Of those who thought they would change, most anticipated a welcome development of character. They felt they would be happier, more confident, less selfish, more tolerant, caring and gentle. They looked forward to being more patient, calmer, responsible and mature, and to a general rounding and fulfilment of their potential.

"I thought it would make me feel more contented and whole as a person, and more satisfied with life as a whole."

"In learning at first hand about how a child develops, I felt I would become a more understanding person, finding out about how people 'tick'."

"I assumed it would make me more mature and responsible, but also help me to rediscover the child in myself!"

"It would bring happiness back into my life. After my first husband died, I didn't want to live."

"I felt I would blossom."

"I knew I would feel more complete – that I'd accomplished something in life and had a real reason for living."

These reactions feel true and right, and seem to come from women who are learning how to be mothers through being in tune with their pregnancy.

A minority of women were less centred on their own development, focussing anxiously instead on how others might see and reject them:

"I was afraid I would be unable to concentrate on anything else and become a baby bore."

"I thought I might become dull and boring, being at home all day."

"I thought I might become mumsy and boring, with nothing to talk about except babies."

It is important to enjoy pregnancy as a time of growth for yourself and your partner. While your baby is developing within you, you have nine months in which to develop into parents. If you can see yourself as growing and developing, you will realize that you have more to offer other people, and not less. For one woman, this came as a pleasant surprise:

"While I was pregnant I felt very insecure, but when my son was born I became more confident. I thought I'd lose my identity, but I didn't."

Again, one or two women had unrealistic expectations of what mother-hood would do for their personalities. A woman who loved her career and loathed domesticity hoped that having a baby would turn her into a contented homebird: it didn't. A woman who had no maternal feelings hoped it would make her "softer": it didn't. And there was a very sad answer from a woman of 21, who wanted a baby "to make me more socially acceptable, and make my family respect me".

Having a baby will enable you to grow and develop those caring quali-ties in yourself which you nourish during pregnancy and as you learn to look after your child: it won't make you into something you are not.

How did you feel when you found out you were pregnant?

A lot of the answers to this question make exciting reading.

"Thrilled and nervous of the unknown."

"I giggled to myself. Couldn't stop grinning. Very excited. Elated, but I knew, or felt I knew, immediately I had conceived."

"Elated. One of the happiest moments of my life."

"Deeply moved and incredulous. Could *my* body actually manage this feat? Smugly content, excited, a bit unsure of the future."

"Stunned after two years of false alarms, delighted, scared."

"Ecstatic. I also felt 'a success' because I had become pregnant so easily."

"I was deliriously happy and elated. I was thrilled and thought I was really clever. I was grinning my face off this planet. I was quite a pain, as I told everybody and anybody I was pregnant."

"Elation, excitement, amazement that there was a little person growing inside me. Also somewhat embarrassed that mum and dad knew we had 'done it'!"

"Wonderful. Elated. I cried for a couple of days in relief."

"Delighted! Good excuse to eat loads."

On discovering that they were pregnant, most women experienced a potent mixture of excitement and tremendous elation mixed with a certain amount of terror – there is a feeling of embarking on a journey into the unknown, from which there is no turning back. There is also often amazement and delight that their bodies have "worked", a sense of incredulity that what usually happens only to other people, has actually happened to them. In fact, it seems little short of a miracle.

In the small minority of cases where getting pregnant was felt to be a disaster, it was always because the event was overshadowed by the feared reaction of another person.

"I was terrified and he was livid."

An unmarried 25-year-old Catholic woman writes:

"I was scared, angry with myself, I felt panicky. I thought: Oh, my God – what will my parents say?"

An unmarried 17-year-old was afraid for her life:

"I really thought I was going to die. My father was very strict and the whole family was afraid of him. I am the eldest of five children and he used to hit us all – most of the time we did not know what for – and when I was 17 he was still hitting me. I honestly thought he would kill me when I found out. He called me a 'bloody fool', but he never hit me again. I did not want my boyfriend, as he was then, to marry me just because he felt he ought to. I felt a great love for my baby right from the start and I was prepared to fight to keep it, even though my parents were talking about having it adopted because there was not room in our house for another child."

Another young woman was so terrified she tried to give herself an abortion:

"I was horrified, as we were living in rented rooms. We both felt shock and terror. We were very young. We were evicted because I was pregnant. I attempted an abortion and failed. We ended up living with my parents, then rented a flat after the birth of the baby."

And in two cases women were devastated when they accidentally conceived on honeymoon with their second husbands. Both already had children from their first marriages and feared that their new husbands would be horrified by another baby, especially so early, but in both cases the husbands turned out to be delighted – one "cried with joy".

 How did your partner react to the news that you were pregnant?

There is quite a difference here between the responses of men who became fathers 20 or 30 years ago and those of younger men. Most men today are as excited and elated at the news as their partners. There is also a strong sense of achievement: the word "proud" cropped up again and again.

"My husband thought he was the bee's knees! He could only brag of his virile prowess. What a boost it was to his ego. He was absolutely delighted and over the moon."

"Happy. Proud that his reproductives were working! Told everybody."

"Proud that he had proved himself, that he had been successful. He wanted to tell everyone immediately. He was very happy."

"Acted like the world's first father!"

"He was very ecstatic. Then he cried and said he was over the moon."

"He says he felt proud of himself and very macho."

"Absolutely thrilled. Wanted to tell the world."

"He pointed at his groin and said: 'It works!'"

One woman, who conceived in the 1960s, threw some interesting light on assumptions made by men at her husband's workplace about childless colleagues that might explain some of the pride and relief:

"I think he was relieved that everything was working as it should, though he didn't actually say so. I remember him saying that the men where he worked made life very hard for those who couldn't have children."

Although we know that the causes of infertility are divided roughly equally between the sexes, and infertility is not the same as impotence, it is evident from the reactions described here that for some men, being able to father a child is deeply felt as the ultimate endorsement of masculinity, just as for some women, fertility is the meaning of femininity. If childless men are still given a hard time at work today, or even if assumptions are made but remain unspoken, it could be truly devastating to be a man and infertile.

Most expert attention in the field of conception, pregnancy and childbirth has focussed, naturally enough, on the woman, and it is only recently that we are coming to realize that men also need sensitive treatment and counselling on such issues as infertility, miscarriage and abortion.

Impatience was another characteristic reaction of men on hearing their partners were pregnant, and it is easy to imagine their eagerness to be more actively involved with the baby growing quietly in the womb. One man had champagne on ice ready for when his wife came home from the doctor's with the news. Another couldn't even wait until the results of the test were confirmed:

"He was delighted! He told my parents even before the pregnancy had been confirmed!"

Another caused his partner a certain amount of alarm by his precipitous reaction:

"Very happy. He rushed straight out and bought a pram. I felt a little uneasy at that, as I thought it was 'tempting fate'."

Sadly, some men were not able to express what they felt. The subdued reaction of the next two men is not typical in the 1990s.

"My partner finds it very hard to be demonstrative, so although I knew he was pleased, I didn't know the depth of his feelings."

"Excited, in a reserved sort of way."

In some cases, women found their husbands' lack of reaction deeply hurtful.

"I don't think he had any feelings. We didn't get emotional about such things in those days."

"I remember he was relaxing on the veranda, reading a book. He showed no outward emotion. I remember how hurt I felt, especially as we had a happy relationship."

And for two women breaking the news was an unforgettable and devastating experience.

"He acted calm, but he said that he would have to work all hours, sell his golf clubs, and cut maintenance to his ex-wife. This made me feel extra scared."

"His first words were: 'Well, as long as it's mine!' – the most hurtful words in my entire life – I have never, ever been unfaithful. My initial joy was totally flattened."

How did pregnancy affect your relationship and your sex life?

This question produced a wide range of answers.

"Pregnancy made us bloom!"

At one end of the scale, couples found the thrill of fertility to be a powerful aphrodisiac. As each revelled in feeling sexually alive and potent, their libido increased, they became more confident, less inhibited and discovered new depths of caring for each other.

"I felt very feminine and our sex drive was just as good – sometimes even better for me, because I felt so feminine."

"He adored me being pregnant. Sex life fine."

"I got very sexy and nearly exhausted my husband! Drew us closer together."

"We remained very close. My sex drive increased enormously, both times."

"We were both very happy and excited. Sex life was enriched. My husband found me particularly attractive. He became very protective, more loving."

"It continued to blossom and I found depths of tenderness and maturity in my husband increasing."

"He nurtured me more. Sex life better."

And for one woman who was aged 16 when she got pregnant:

"It didn't change – we were still at it night and day."

It often happens that women discover themselves sexually for the first time during pregnancy, because the changes they are living through make them more aware of and in tune with the way their bodies work.

Some women also mention the liberating side-effects of being pregnant. One says how happy she was to be free of PMT, and that pregnancy enhanced all aspects of her relationship and her sex life; another that sex improved because she and her partner no longer had to worry about contraception. Several say that as pregnancy progressed and they needed to find more comfortable positions, sex became more inventive and imaginative.

"When it was uncomfortable in one position, we tried another. We were certainly not inhibited. As for our relationship, we felt the pregnancy sealed our love and we were really excited to become parents. We were so happy during my pregnancy."

For those who had problem-free pregnancies, the nine months is remembered as a time of blossoming, and of feeling truly cherished.

Pregnancy and not feeling like sex

Other women were not so lucky with their health, and their sex lives were not so active.

"I was ill through most of my pregnancy, so sex was not uppermost in our minds."

But where the relationship was already good and close, feeling unwell was not an obstacle to getting closer. On the contrary, many couples found that if love could not be expressed sexually, it could still grow and deepen in other ways.

"A closeness developed. He took a more caring role, looking after me. Sex became less frequent."

"We had a happy relationship and my husband was very caring and understanding when sex wasn't possible."

It is quite common to feel nausea in the first three months, and whether this is accompanied by actual vomiting or not, it is not likely to put you in the mood for making love. What is important at this time is to feel that your partner understands what is happening to you and that he can give you a lot of emotional support and love. Physical affection in the form of cuddling up in bed, holding, stroking and reassurance, is more important now than sexual love.

One man, who was very much in tune with his wife's pregnancy writes:

"I think it brought us closer. As the pregnancy progressed I wanted to do more for my wife so she could take things easier. We didn't have sex quite as often, but we realised this would only be temporary."

For one couple who had both suffered abuse as children, abstaining from sex during pregnancy took a lot of the pressure out of their relationship and allowed them to grow together in what both felt to be a non-threatening atmosphere:

"We grew closer during pregnancy. Due to past experiences on both sides, sex was terrible anyway, so I was happy to be pregnant and not need to have sex."

Can sex harm the baby?

In some cases, women who were in danger of miscarrying were advised to abstain from sex by their doctors. One woman describes how she and her husband survived the frustrations of a sexless pregnancy, and more frustration after the birth:

"I miscarried after 12 weeks, but became pregnant again six weeks later. At about 10 weeks I began to bleed slightly and my doctor told me to avoid sex until the 15th week. I found after that time I just couldn't bring myself to risk losing the baby by making love. My husband was incredibly understanding and put up with my irrational behaviour until the birth. After my son was born I was badly sewn up (by a locum) and so dreadfully sore that I couldn't bear to be penetrated for four months. I felt miserable not being able to make love when we both wanted to, especially after my 'no sex' pregnancy. Everyone tells you that you are able to have sex a few weeks after the birth – I had no idea that I wouldn't be able to for so long."

It's interesting that this woman calls her fear of miscarrying "irrational" and is grateful to her husband for putting up with her behaviour. Surely her fears were quite resonable, given her medical history. "Irrational" is a word that men traditionally use to describe women who are reacting to instinctive feelings – it's a put-down. Sadly, women have adopted the male view of themselves and tend to apologize and blame themselves for insights and instincts that are often, as here, perfectly justified.

Under normal circumstances there is usually no medical reason why a couple should abstain from sex at any stage of pregnancy. Penetration of the vagina cannot touch, let alone harm the baby, who is safe in the womb. The bag of waters that encloses the baby cushions it from knocks so that even if the abdomen is bumped hard, it will merely bounce back into position. There is a plug of mucus at the neck of the womb that provides an additional seal.

As the baby grows inside her, the woman will obviously find certain positions for making love uncomfortable. Lying underneath her partner, she will feel crushed, unless he raises himself right off her with his weight on his arms, and penetration will become difficult for him, too.

Try other positions, such as penetration from behind, both lying on your sides, or on all fours; or the woman can sit on her partner's lap, or astride his body as he lies on the bed. Towards the end of pregnancy, if she is feeling very cumbersome, oral sex and mutual masturbation may be more satisfying.

But even if you have been reassured by your doctor that sex will not harm the baby, and even if you accept, logically, that it won't, you may still harbour fears that make you reluctant to have sex.

"I withdrew and was very involved in what was happening to my body. Sex life was almost non-existent because I thought it might affect the baby. I know better now that it couldn't have."

"As the bump grew I felt it should not be crushed and was unwilling to participate in what I believed were damaging positions."

"Pregnancy did our relationship harm to begin with. I did not want to be touched. Thought intercourse would harm the baby."

"Our sex life was not very good and it did not improve. I think he was fearful of damaging the baby."

"Abstained first couple of months due to threatened miscarriage. Didn't enjoy sex after that – felt wrong psychologically (silly, I know)."

As long as both of you feel happier about not having sex and can remain close, it really does not matter that your reasons for abstaining are illogical. But problems start when one person's reluctance to make love causes the other person to feel rejected.

Pregnancy and rejection

Some women were understandably very hurt when their partners made it clear that they no longer found them attractive.

"I felt he had little or no consideration for me, and no great joy. He was *not* excited by the pregnant form of [a] woman – even one he was supposed to be in love with. I felt empty and alone and unacknowledged."

"My being 'fat' put my partner off sex somewhat."

"Pregnancy affected us disastrously. He refused to take me out or even buy maternity wear for me. I had to haunt jumble sales. Sex life – forget it. He didn't find a fat cow, elephant (take your pick) attractive, and told me so."

"My husband said I was moodier than ever. Our sex life was non-existent. My husband had to tell me that he didn't find pregnant women sexually attractive."

The rejection from other men was more subtle, but nonetheless disturbing.

"Towards the end when I got larger, my husband found it 'offputting'. My daughter was very active in my womb and he could feel her kicking even when he just cuddled me."

"Husband did not like touching my bump, especially when the baby was moving, which I would like to have shared with him."

"I wanted my husband to be more interested in things like feeling the baby kick."

This apparent squeamishness about the unborn baby moving inside his partner's body may conceal a feeling that is more difficult for the father-to-be to confront. One woman diagnoses it as jealousy, and for her it explains not only her husband's hurtful lack of sexual interest, but also his illogical explanation that he didn't want to hurt their unborn twins.

"Looking back, I think my husband started to feel a bit jealous when I was a few months pregnant, at the thought that I had someone else to consider already. Our sex life did start to dwindle when I got bigger, even though I was still keen. My husband kept saying he didn't want to hurt our babies, and even though I assured him that was nonsense, he still didn't seem interested. I felt quite hurt emotionally, but he does not like discussing feelings very much. The first half of my pregnancy was wonderful, but I think he was irritated by some of the discomforts I experienced, such as intense itching all over my body, which was worse in bed at night. My husband chose not to sleep separately from me but offered little sympathy."

A man who rejects his partner during pregnancy may well be doing so to protect himself against the rejection he fears from her. To many men, the relationship between the mother and the unborn child seems so complete that they feel excluded. With the interest of friends and relatives and all the medical attention focussed on his partner, an insecure man may feel as though he is no longer needed, no longer important or even useful. The pregnancy is seen as a threat to his own status, so he reacts by cutting off to defend himself against hurt. As jealousy is not an easy emotion to acknowledge, particularly with regard to your own unborn child, it often manifests itself as something more acceptable, such as squeamishness, or fear of hurting the baby with penetration, or sheer inability to cope.

"What with my tiredness and feeling constantly sick for three months, and having aversions to red meat, tea and coffee, and working full time – he couldn't cope with it all."

"There is no doubt that pregnancy caused him to be very irritable, especially when pressures at work were a problem to him."

In extreme cases, a man who feels redundant at home will feel the need to prove himself elsewhere.

"During the first pregnancy I was sick, so our sex life must have suffered. During my second pregnancy my husband went off and had an affair."

It is very understandable when women take their partners' rejections at face value and react against them. After all, the woman is in a vulnerable position and needs supporting and protecting. But a wise woman will show her partner how much she needs and wants him, and will make him feel that the pregnancy belongs to both of them, so that his jealousy and fear of rejection will, it is hoped, slip away.

It is only relatively recently that men have become involved in child-birth and in looking after their own children. Both sexes are still unused to the fact that men and women are moving closer together. Women are new to sharing what used to be a totally female experience, and men are new to taking that share. Men need to be made to feel welcome.

One woman describes how her confidence in her new husband won through in a difficult situation, when he feared that the child she had conceived accidentally would come between them:

"We had been together a year and it was an unplanned pregnancy. I was 30, my husband was 40, and we already had five children between us (two mine and three his). My husband was very unhappy and sometimes angry that this had happened so early in our marriage and was relaying to me feelings that were very out of character. He would have had me have an abortion and said he would have nothing to do with the child when it was born. I knew he would soften up later on."

Can making love trigger labour?
"We made love right until I went into labour. It was that that started it off."

If you are ready to go into labour, and especially if you are to be induced, making love may help start it off. The uterus contracts during orgasm, as it does during labour, but having an orgasm will not trigger labour unless you are ready for it. Prostaglandins, which are present in semen, also cause contractions of the uterus. If you lie on your back with your legs raised around your partner's hips, he will be able to ejaculate right at the cervix. As this position may be uncomfortable so late in pregnancy, proceed very gently.

It's important to realize that having sex will not cause you to go into labour unless you are ready to do so. It is safe to have sex right up to the end of pregnancy, unless your doctor advises otherwise. You would be advised to abstain if you have had premature labour before, or if you have blood spotting, or the cervical mucus plug has been dislodged, as this would allow the possibility of infection.

CHILDBIRTH

This question elicited some of the longest and most detailed answers. They make fascinating reading, especially for anyone whose experience of childbirth has been gained at second hand through reading manuals.

Q. Describe your experience of childbirth.

Finding out all you can about giving birth from books and from other people will provide useful preparation for the event, but no one can tell you quite what it will be like for you. There is no standard for giving birth by which to measure yourself, and no such thing as success or failure. It is important to remember that your own experience belongs uniquely to you — it will take you somewhere you have never been before and is yours to live and to keep.

In the accounts that follow, pain, frustration, fear and overwhelming joy are all vividly remembered.

To begin with, here is an account from 1953, in the days when men were not allowed into the delivery ward. The mother is a young Catholic woman, who went on from the traumatic experience she describes here to give birth to eight more children.

"The reception was a bit daunting, especially when they shaved me. The nurse said: 'Oh dear, the razor is rusty!' I was given an enema and told to walk down a long corridor to the loo. I began to feel distinctly unhappy and rather frightened! After my husband left that evening when visitors' hours were over they told me to go into a side ward with a labour bed that was virtually too high for me to get on to! That night I spent in absolute fear. I clutched my rosary, but couldn't pray. The light shone into the room from the street lamp outside the window. Every little twinge I thought was one of the pains I needed to have if I was to produce this baby. I didn't sleep a wink. Many was the time I thought I would press the alarm bell for the nurse to come, but was too frightened to. At dawn I was offered kippers for breakfast and they brought me a cup of liquid paraffin! I won't tell you what I thought of that!

[Eventually, after she was sick all over the doctor's suit,] they strung up my legs and gave me an anaesthetic and the baby was delivered by forceps. I had to be cut, and a particularly long cut! My husband was in the waiting room. They showed him the baby, who hadn't been washed and was marked from the forceps. He took one look and fainted! The nurse told him later that I had been praying whilst under the anaesthetic! I learned that my mother and father, plus friends at our church were on their knees for me and baby to come through safely.

I had some very uncomfortable stitches of gut underneath me, the ends of which were knotted together; they made sitting most uncomfortable. I remember the staff being mightily concerned because I hadn't passed urine after the birth and they were all around me with taps running, trying to get me to do so! I felt so wretched!

This was the physical suffering, but there was mental suffering too. My husband couldn't visit me after the birth because the doctor suspected he had the mumps! Not only he, but my parents were put in quarantine, as well as my brothers. I felt so unhappy. The three weeks I was in hospital was a traumatic time, and I felt very lonely."

This next account shows how restrictive giving birth in hospital still was in the 1960s to both parents, and how much the couple benefited from sharing subsequent births.

"Way back then [1960s], the babies were kept in a nursery in order to allow the mothers to rest. During the nine days that I was in the hospital, my son was only ever brought to me to be fed, and I bathed him only once before I went home.

When my husband came to visit, the nurses had to throw him out. He was so thrilled with his son that he would quite happily have stood there all day just looking at him. He was always the first in the nursery, and the last out.

Our two subsequent children were both home deliveries and my husband was present for the whole of the labour and the births. He enjoyed being with me and we still laugh at the funny things that happened, such as having to dispose of the afterbirth and having it sizzle on the fire all night. Having a baby at home is a much more relaxed experience and I was pleased to have my husband's support and encouragement."

Since men have been allowed in the delivery room, most couples ask for the father to be present at the birth, and in the vast majority of cases this turns out to be the right decision for both parents. The following accounts speak for themselves.

"Good experience. I had a very quick and easy time. My partner was with me throughout and was very supportive. It was the most emotional thing that has ever happened to us both and it brought us closer together."

"[Mrs:] It was a novelty! It was nothing like I'd experienced before. Hard work. Very emotionally charged (a moving experience, feelings of excitement, anticipation, very tiring, very joyful eventually), never felt closer to my husband than during labour.

[Mr:] We had both attended NCT [National Childbirth Trust] classes, so I was there and I wouldn't have missed it! I felt overjoyed at the actual births themselves, moved, emotional, but also useful because I could help her through the various stages. It did bring us close and we finished as we had started – as a partnership – a winning team."

"My partner was there from start to finish. He was completely overwhelmed and emotional. Made us extremely close and humorous – he still mocks my behaviour in labour (sissy, he says!)."

"My husband hadn't been allowed to be present at the births of his first family. I wouldn't have liked to be on my own. I enjoyed the delivery but would have liked a little more time for the three of us to be together immediately afterwards. The experience brought us very close, both as a couple and as a family."

"He was pretty impressed – quite squeamish the first time – brought us very close together – cried, with joy and stuff. Nos. 2 and 3 were quite fun, as we knew exactly what was happening."

"The day I gave birth to my daughter was the best in my whole life – it was wonderful. I had a very straightforward labour and delivery and experienced all of it without any pain relief (which I was determined not to have). My husband was very supportive and with me throughout labour and delivery. He was a bit nervous, but me being a midwife helped, because I could tell him exactly what was going on. I was touched that he was so overwhelmed when I gave birth to my daughter and couldn't seem to believe such a miracle for days afterwards."

"When I had my first baby – it was the happiest day of my life. Cried with joy. My partner was present throughout and also cried. We felt very close. He thought the birth was wonderful."

"Childbirth was a family experience. It was at home with not only my husband present, but also my mother and two midwives I knew well. Apart from the discomfort, it was a happy experience that I felt everyone shared with me."

"My blood pressure shot up, so I was on gas and air and pethidine. Painful and it lasted eight hours, short for a first one. My partner was present. At one point I remember him eating a pasty! He was very supportive and I listened to him rather than to the medical staff. He cut the cord and he had tears in his eyes as he handed me our son. He was also present at the second, which was much easier. Again he cut the cord and again he cried. 'Best experience of my life,' was how he put it."

"I couldn't have done it without him. He was wonderful both times – very supportive and encouraging throughout. His words were: 'The end product is marvellous, but I wish I hadn't seen you go through so much pain.'"

"I found giving birth not as bad as I had expected. I was very calm all the way through, helped by my husband. Every so often he would say: 'You're alright,' and I would think, yes I am. He seemed to know what to do."

"Brought us very close. Felt 'solidified' as a family unit."

"He found it a great experience. It was a completely shared event. I found his support vital."

For most contributors, the second time they gave birth was easier than the first:

"The birth of our second child was quite different. I'd had a pregnancy that ended in miscarriage at three months, but I sailed through the next one. When the baby was 10 days overdue, I went into labour at 3 am. I got up and had several cuppas, breathed through the contractions, crouched on the floor and did all I could to relieve the pain, which was not unbearable like the first time. The baby was born three hours later, 20 minutes after we got to hospital. There was no time for any painkillers, but it wasn't too bad. The urge to push that time was much greater than before, and apparently I contorted my face and grunted so much etc. that my husband said: 'That's it – I'll never put you through that again.' I felt that the whole thing had been a doddle! During the first labour, frankly, I couldn't have cared less whether my husband had been there or not, but the second time around we had lots of hugs between contractions, and laughed a lot because we knew we'd got to the hospital only just in time."

For some couples, the experience of childbirth released strong and lasting emotions.

"He said it was an indescribable and unique feeling and very powerful, so much that you are on a high for hours afterwards. I would say it brought us closer together."

"It was a beautiful birth. I felt very calm. Everything went well. It was an active childbirth. He was present, as was his mum. I think he was nervous – excited and apprehensive together. The childbirth brought us extremely close. It released so many emotions between us that haven't disappeared since – in fact they have increased."

"At the second birth my husband was with me throughout and this was a wonderful experience for us both, and has lasted throughout our marriage."

One woman describes the difference her husband's presence made, and how the pain was much less bearable when she delivered her second baby without him. Research bears out her observations.

"I didn't want anybody to see my face and I hid beneath a Habitat facecloth. It was vanity on my part. My husband was so excited he couldn't care less. He gave me a running commentary of the descending head. He was flushed with the whole experience. When the baby was born, we both shed tears of joy. We both felt so fulfilled. It is funny how my husband felt that he had actually gone through the whole labour himself. Our feelings when we both held our son for the first time were tumultuous.

With my son's birth I stifled my pain to be brave for my husband, but with the second birth I was alone, and the painkillers were not effective. Nurses do not comfort in the same way a partner can!"

Several women who did not have a good experience of childbirth say that their husbands gave them vital support. Difficult births shared also brought couples closer. The first account comes from a nurse, and shows that no amount of training can prepare you for the real thing.

"I had a difficult birth and some post-natal depression. My husband was very supportive. We were both very anxious with our first baby."

"It wasn't the wonderful experience I had imagined it to be. I was very, very frightened. I couldn't believe that so much pain was normal, and was convinced that something was wrong. My husband was with me throughout, very patient and supportive."

"Childbirth not good. Induced. Epidural (thank goodness!), baby in wrong position – double forceps Keiland rotation delivery as child in distress after nine hours. Partner present throughout. Most concerned and highly relieved when child delivered safely. Experience brought us closer."

"Frightening and very painful. It had been described as a bad period pain – it was far, far worse. The nurses expected me to know exactly what I was doing. My husband was with me and he was very supportive. I felt him being there made us very close."

"I was very ill, which induced an early birth. Fortunately the birth was normal and we supported each other, having done NCT classes together. Our son was desperately ill with a 50 per cent chance of survival and it closened our relationship during a very traumatic time."

"I was frightened. My partner was worried as he didn't realize it would be so painful. It did bring us very close."

"I was very disappointed when my son was born (three and a half weeks early), because he was very squashed. It took me a few days, with my husband's support, to feel very motherly. My daughter, who arrived a fortnight late, was totally different. I couldn't believe how beautiful she was. I still feel guilty when I think how I felt then."

A man's calming influence can even be felt at long distance, according to one woman:

"My husband [a nurse at that time] was very laid-back about my confinement. I was over-anxious, away from my family. I think his calmness helped me. If he had panicked, so would I. He organized the ambulance, and then left for work – at another hospital!"

And in one case, even though the man was so affected that he had to leave the room, his caring gave his wife the support she needed:

"With the first birth my husband was not there and I felt very lonely. He was present at the second birth but is not very good in that sort of situation and had to leave the room. I did find it brought us closer, his being there during the very last stages of labour. I felt very secure."

Men who don't get involved

Men may feel useless in the face of the pain their partners are suffering, but as long as they are in tune with the pain and alive to the experience, their presence is the best possible support.

Men who attend the birth but don't allow themselves to be vulnerable to what is happening are no help at all. This very small minority of men have either already distanced themselves from their wives as a first stage of leaving, or are possibly too frightened of witnessing pain to allow themselves to be affected. In some cases there may also be an element of guilt involved – a desire to hide from the suffering for which they feel responsible.

Several women mentioned their irritation at a husband who couldn't give his full attention to labour. One man nipped back and forth from his office all day, giving the impression that his work took priority; another was always popping off to the hospital canteen for a cup of tea, and a third kept rushing off for a smoke. One woman's husband was gleeful because he nearly missed the birth while he was at a football match:

"On the day my first son was born my husband was at Wembley at a football match. I was alone all day, frightened by what was happening to me. Eventually the midwife came and I was rushed into hospital with high blood pressure. My husband arrived in time for the birth. He thought it was a high joke, him not being there for me, although he did think the birth was marvellous."

Two held themselves completely aloof from the proceedings:

"Childbirth was painful, cold, basic. Husband present but he and I felt he was detached. Drove a wedge between us. I felt totally alone."

"My partner was present and said: 'She is making a big show of this.' He didn't understand why I wouldn't cooperate with the midwife's advice on breathing and he never will understand because he is a man. I certainly did feel very alone during the birth – my partner preferred to tell me to stop screaming and shouting rather than help me calm down."

131

One woman perhaps unfairly blames her husband. If she had given vent to her feelings, he might have appreciated them better:

"I felt my husband did not appreciate what I was going through. I suppressed the screams because he was there. At the end he said: 'That wasn't too bad, was it?' I think childbirth is hell."

And this woman's husband, though present, had already left her in spirit for someone else:

"He was by then very distant and already running – infatuated with another lady. There in body, but absent. A real feeling of going it alone. And that was very sad."

For two women, who were not in tune with either their pregnancies or their men, it was a dreadfully low point in their lives and in their relationships:

"I hated the childbirth, it was undignified, ugly and painful. I didn't understand or relate to my own body. My husband was with me and I blamed him. I thought I would never be the same afterwards. He accepted everything I threw at him and never expressed shock or hurt."

"I felt horrifically embarrassed. I didn't want him in the labour ward. I found the whole experience disgusting and terrifying."

Finally, here is a truly awful story from a woman married to a very callous husband who currently has a high-ranking job in the prison service.

"My second baby was a breech birth (feet first), and I went to hell and back. I would have loved my husband to be with me. I really did feel as if I was on my own. I always wanted another baby to see if I could have a daughter. My husband just would not consider it and this did a lot of damage to our relationship. He worked long hours and did not seem to care what I was feeling. Two years after my second son was born I had to have a tidying-up operation – a D & C – because I had had so much damage that I kept getting infections. Our sex life was not good. After this operation – I was on the Pill and I did not forget to take them – I had a false pregnancy, where I had a placenta but not a foetus. The doctor thought it might have been caused by a hormonal imbalance. I was thought to be 'pregnant' for five months. My husband was really terrible at this time and most unsupportive. He knew I had not forgotten to take the Pill, but could not come to terms with my 'pregnancy'. When I had a 'miscarriage' he celebrated. This was the start of a really low period in our marriage. I really did feel alone."

Caesarean section

Predictably, the women who have had both a Caesarean section and a "normal" delivery, prefer the latter.

"Awful! I had a Caesarean first time. My partner was present, but due to an allergic reaction during the op., I was subsequently very ill and in no state to think about feelings. Second time was a normal delivery. I enjoyed the whole thing, as did my husband. We spent the whole day together, which was a novelty! We laughed and cried together, and I couldn't have done it without him."

"My first delivery was very traumatic to both myself and my daughter. My husband was there the whole time and was very good at helping me to breathe properly, push and so on. Our bonding process with our daughter was immediate. We both cried and were so overwhelmed with pride at having produced a new person who was so perfect. With the second baby I had a Caesarean and a general anaesthetic. My husband wasn't allowed in. Our bonding took a lot longer and the immense relief and achievement [weren't] there."

Though partners are usually asked to leave if there are complications and the baby is to be born by Caesarean, in some cases they may be allowed to stay. It usually depends on the level of distress involved, and how the husband is coping with it. It is not necessary for your partner to watch if he prefers not to, as a screen surrounds the operation and he can stand by your head and give you emotional support.

If you know in advance that you are going to have a Caesarean, and you decide you do want to share the birth, discuss it with your obstetrician. If he or she tries to dissuade you and you still want to go ahead, you may be able to arrange to have the birth at another hospital.

Two couples who wanted to share a Caesarean delivery found it a rewarding experience:

"I had an elective Caesarean, and my husband was present. He was very supportive and involved, taking photos etc. He wept when the baby was born. I was moved by his emotion. The experience made us feel very close."

133

"My husband was present. It took all day and all night, and eventually I had a Caesarean under anaesthetic – it wasn't the pleasurable experience I had looked forward to. The surgeon said he would write on the palm of my hand what sex it was and when I awoke the next day in a haze, I saw very faintly 'girl' on my palm, and 'knew' everything was fine. My husband was very loving."

If complications arise, the mother and baby may not be reunited after the birth for some time.

"I had a difficult labour, the baby was in distress and I had to have an emergency Caesarean section under general anaesthetic – the epidural hadn't worked properly. Then I had a tear on the lining of my womb and lost a lot of blood during the operation, so had to go into intensive care for 24 hours to be monitored and given blood. I didn't see my daughter for eight hours and couldn't nurse her or care for her until two days later. She was healthy with no after-effects from the distressed stage before birth."

One woman had twins by Caesarean, and while she was too ill to travel, the babies had to be rushed to a special care unit over 100 miles away in London. Every day for a week, her husband drove up to see them and came back to tell her how they were doing. Despite the distress and anxiety that this situation must have caused, her husband has given her a very positive memory of that time. She writes: "He was wonderful throughout."

Most would share this woman's happiness that her husband's involvement made them a family despite the separation. Knowing your baby is being cared for by someone who loves her gives a feeling of warmth and security that is very important at this vulnerable stage. But one woman did not see it like this and was resentful:

"I had a horrendous labour with my husband present, but then had to have an emergency Caesarean. I then felt he had the pleasure of getting to know our little girl while I suffered the after-effects of a general anaesthetic."

In another case, it was the other way around, with the husband feeling cheated of being at the birth because his wife went into premature labour without him:

"I was to have elective Caesarean for foot breech and didn't mind about this. Three weeks before term I went away to a conference with full medical approval. Into labour on the last day – emergency Caesarean (baby and me fine!) Husband whizzed up on train and we both saw baby for the first time together. He seemed to find the whole thing highly amusing but later I found out he was furious with me."

Surprisingly, only one woman voiced the classic complaint that a Caesarean robs you of the experience of "doing it yourself", and leaves you feeling as though you have somehow failed.

"I had a Caesarean section. My experience was not good. I didn't feel elated after the birth – I couldn't have cared less. I felt I had been deprived of the satisfaction of giving birth."

Complaints about hospital births

The majority of births described by women in this survey took place in hospital, but the hospital routine and surroundings were rarely mentioned: memories were more intimately focussed. However, for a handful of women, hospital was not a good experience. This account comes from a woman who is herself a nurse:

"The birth was very long (28 hours). Left for long periods with few nursing staff (as a nurse, I was supercritical!), hated the whole experience, wanted to die and never have another baby! Husband stayed with me the whole time, but did not enjoy the experience. Did it for me, not out of choice. However, in retrospect, it enhanced our relationship. The second birth was at home – much better – a totally different experience."

In this case, lack of attention was the complaint. In another, the nursing staff figured too largely, depersonalizing the whole experience.

"I felt very much on my own though my husband was with me. The nursing staff had everything in their control and I felt that my feelings were not being taken into consideration. Once the baby was born – a normal delivery after 36 hours – I did not see her until the next morning."

Another woman resented having to give way to the authority of the doctor over painkillers, when she had wanted a natural childbirth:

"The first time, I hated childbirth – it was very long and very painful, which I had told myself wouldn't happen. Wanted a natural birth, but felt a failure, because it did hurt. I begged not to have drugs, but the doctor overrode me. I was angry with my partner for not standing up to the doctor. The second time was great though. We were more assertive and less frightened, and I coped better. My partner hated the experience as he couldn't bear to see my pain. He felt it was all very clinical. He was there because I'd asked him to be there. I was glad he was there because I could swear at him."

This woman also coped better the second time around:

"The gas and air somehow made me delirious so I did not have a meaningful experience. I was unaware of my husband's presence. He thought it was wonderful to watch and that every man should have the experience. The second child took only three hours and I needed no gas, so this was truly a very moving experience for me, and him too, because I was totally aware of him."

PARENTHOOD

This chapter gives a welter of different views of parenthood – the real-life first-hand experience is fascinating and could prove more useful to new parents than the official guidelines in many a baby or childcare manual. The parents who write here are as honest about their own doubts and feelings of inadequacy as they are about the positive aspects of having children. They talk about post-natal depression and problems with feeding, and later about problems with discipline. Again it emerges that men's failure to share parenthood is a major cause of the breakdown of marriage.

Q: What were the main pleasures and problems you experienced in looking after your baby and yourselves during the first few weeks of your baby's life?

For the parents, the first weeks of their baby's life are crowded and vivid with new experiences. It is an exhausting time that brings both anxiety and great joy. Many answers reflect both the excitement and the sheer hard work involved in becoming parents.

"Trying to get into some sort of routine seemed virtually impossible. Never seemed to get dressed until lunchtime! It was a real pleasure to see my partner handle such a tiny little thing and to see so much love in his eyes."

"First 10 days were bliss – cocooned together – then he went back to work and baby had colic for 3 months! Mild post-natal depression set in!"

"Enchantment of holding a little miracle in one's arms – the soft warm baby smell and the closeness of breastfeeding – and sharing all this with my partner. Problems with living in a very isolated place, and realising that this [child] was for life. Also, she suffered from screaming colic every evening for six months."

"The main problems were the responsibility for this new life and the utter exhaustion we both felt. The pleasures were more subtle. The small hand clutching your finger. The way she quietenend when you held her. The wonderful love that grew with her. The way she needed you."

137

"The first birth brought us very close together. With the others, he was supportive during the birth, but much less so afterwards [he only wanted one child]. I resented his refusal to change a nappy. However, he helped a lot with cooking and shopping, also housework. My main pleasures were cuddling the baby and breastfeeding, which I loved."

"Total and overwhelming feelings of utter and absolute love and joy with our new son. But baby was a poor sleeper and poor feeder – both exhausted. Very isolated – no shops or close friends or family nearby. We had no money and darkness and cold in small hours ([during] feeding times etc.) made me miserable."

"Cuddling my baby and breastfeeding him. I felt very close and protective. He was a difficult baby, never slept well, did not feed well and cried a lot. I felt anxious and wanted to be the 'perfect' mother."

"Loved the arrival of each new milestone – first smile, lifting head, sitting up etc. Husband very proud and interested. Lack of sleep and complete disruption of routine and inability to cope with day-to-day running of the house."

"Cradling a small baby in your arms; giving security and love and total care and responsibility. The main problem was with two-hourly breastfeeding, which meant that my husband had to cook, clean etc. when he came in from work. I acted very strangely towards him, though no one commented on it at the time. I definitely gave my husband a hard time."

"Found it difficult to keep asking for simple things like 'pass a nappy', or 'shoot upstairs for that pillow' when I was used to doing things for myself. Main pleasure – this fantastic bundle was our pride and joy – our product of unity, if you like."

Sheer joy

For a lucky few, there were either no problems at all, or they felt so happy to be parents that they hardly noticed them.

"Sheer joy. Breastfeeding was probably the greatest pleasure. My husband [who had already had children by his first wife] was more confident handling the baby at bathtimes, dressing etc. than I was, so we were both totally involved. The biggest surprise was how protective I felt towards the baby. I was too happy to see any problems."

"There were no real problems. I was very lucky in that my new baby slept when he should and ate when he should. He was a very happy baby."

"We felt extreme happiness about this new life. For me it was a feeling of contentment and feeling secure that everything had worked out right after my first marriage break-up. My son was a very contented baby. My daughter [by first marriage] seemed more secure. Everything ran smoothly."

"I felt very happy and fulfilled and every moment was a joy."

"Everything was wonderful. We glowed. We were even more in love. Found it difficult to wait the six weeks before the postnatal examination."

"Great sense of completeness and love. Realizing we could cope as parents with only a little money and a poorly equipped home. Lack of sleep!"

"Despite colic and lack of sleep, we were both so totally buoyed up that we floated around for weeks after."

Men who took an active role

For many women, the fact that their partner took an active role was crucial to their enjoyment of motherhood. Some say they could not have coped without his physical and emotional support.

When the father becomes involved in looking after his baby and the running of the house — as much as his work allows — it creates a secure family bond. Feeling part of a team takes the worst of the stress and anxiety out of looking after even the most difficult baby, because you know there is someone else who cares as much as you do, who will take as much pleasure in seeing your baby develop, and who can take over when you're too tired to do any more.

One man describes what seems like an ideal first two weeks:

"I had two weeks off work – time devoted to each other cementing the family bond. The chores were set aside – we had the excuse to do nothing but rest and look after the baby. Pleasures of holding, cuddling, feeding the baby. Problems: sleepless nights, crying."

Several women remember the satisfaction of sharing babycare with their partners:

"We used to share the baby's routine bathing and feeding. The only thing that I remember doing more than my husband was nappy changing. He is left-handed and he always looked so awkward trying to do up the pin on those thick towelling nappies."

"I had problems putting on the baby's nappies safely, but my partner showed me how as he'd done it all before."

"We decided that it was vital to make time for *us*, so from day one the baby would have a bedtime, and get up at breakfast time. So after the 6pm feed she went to bed in her room, and my partner or I (thank God for the breast pump!) would go and feed her at 10pm/2am, whether she was awake or not, then get her up at breakfast time. This we did having watched friends who had no routines at all going nuts, having no time without the baby, and having houses where nappies and bibs oozed out of every room."

"Delight in having this wonderful new being in our lives, and to see my husband's delight in her too. Problems were getting enough sleep (both of us), and for me, feeling helpless during sleepless nights when my husband was working on night duty. Quite often my partner would take our daughter out for two hours when he got back tired from his night shift, so I could sleep, before going to bed himself. I was very wrapped up with our daughter, and finding time to do the normal things – like getting meals ready on time – was very difficult."

"Our main problem was lack of privacy, living with parents. My husband looked after me very well – meals, shopping etc. Before we had the baby I wondered what we'd do if it cried all the time, as I didn't think either of us would be any good. When she cried with colic, I'd feel useless and tend to get upset, but my husband would sweep her away and walk round the garden with her until she stopped. I would feel that he knew me well – better than I'd thought. He knew when he could get away with joking, or if I was really down."

"Very exciting – very tiring! I was exhausted with night feeds. My husband helped – otherwise I couldn't have coped. At first I felt very unsure and inadequate."

"After my son's birth I was very poorly in hospital for 10 days. My husband had the first four weeks off work and did everything – meals, housework, shopping, ironing, prepared the milk feeds and got up in the night to our baby. I enjoyed taking over when I was strong enough. The early weeks are all nappies, feeds and feeling very tired, but it soon changes. Now I look back with affection at those weeks and I would like another baby, but my husband is happy with two."

"No sleep. Painful breastfeeding. Husband wonderful. Cooked, cleaned, helped with breastfeeding and went to work."

And two men describe their own involvement:

"I enjoyed taking my turn at feeding time. I was also in charge of the nappy bucket. No problems to speak of."

"I was afraid to hold her and change her for the first week, but then I did as much as I could."

Men who withdrew from mother and baby

For some women, the most distressing problem in the weeks following the birth was that their partners withdrew, making them feel they were going it totally alone. One man began by helping, but his involvement was short-lived.

"For two weeks he did everything – cooked, shopped, cleaned etc. – so I could deal with baby. Then it was back to normal and I had to do everything. He wouldn't touch baby."

Some men acted as if nothing had changed. They were oblivious of the baby and of the demands it made on their wives, and expected life to go on just as before.

"The main problem was that my husband expected everything to carry on as before, smoothly and without interrupting routine, which was, of course, impossible."

"My husband felt that life was just the same and continued in his normal pattern. I was tired and felt the responsibility of the world on my shoulders. I didn't feel in tune with my son – he didn't look like I had expected. I cried and worried a lot."

"In hospital you feel safe looking after the baby, but coming home was frightening, as the responsibility hit me. Nights were very draining and he

141

left it all to me to deal with. He made it clear that he wasn't good at dealing with dirty nappies and his life was not affected at all. This period was not shared and it caused problems."

"I felt I had something that actually belonged to me and that I could call my own. I felt tired and irritable most of the time because my partner did not help in any way. I still have two babies to look after [him and her daughter]."

In some instances, the new father had a negative reaction to his baby.

"Husband [displayed] occasional unbelievable hostility, e.g. if disturbed by baby in middle of night. But on the whole not too bad."

"From the very beginning my husband was frightened of the baby and reluctant even to hold him. I was in a lot of pain after a long, painful forceps delivery and wanted him to help and share in looking after the baby. He could only help with household chores and avoided me when I was with the baby. My husband was embarrassed at my breastfeeding."

"Few pleasures except love for my new son. Problems set in immediately with my husband. He felt neglected and threatened, completely without cause."

"My husband begrudged having to visit me in hospital. I was in for 10 days. On reflection he was the baby that had been replaced and he behaved like it. He would not speak or help me."

"There were difficulties in the evening when the baby would cry and my husband insisted that he stay in his bedroom. I would sit on the stairs and cry with him."

Sometimes, the man's inability to cope with the reality of fatherhood drove him out of the house, leaving his wife bewildered and weighed down with responsibility.

"I was on my own. He didn't know anything about babies and didn't want to. My babies' needs were more important than his because he wouldn't do anything for them. He disliked the role he was forced to play. He went out drinking and played golf."

"I don't recall the first few weeks, even months, of our son's life as being at all pleasurable, as my partner thought it was an excuse to be out all day and night drinking with his friends, and as our son was not a very happy baby, i.e. he didn't sleep for longer than two hours, I felt under great pressure."

"The main problem I think was no mum or mother-in-law to rely on – but we managed. I remember crying for my mum, who died when I was 9½. I just wanted her to see my daughter. I was also very hurt and disappointed when my husband went off to play in his band three days after the birth; overall, though, it was a lovely time. I was a bit overawed when I realized I was totally responsible for the welfare of the child – never again 'free' as I once had been."

It would seem that these men all felt to a greater or lesser degree threatened. They felt the baby usurped their own place in their wives' affections. Withdrawal is a form of self-defence. If you shove your head in the sand and carry on as normal, pretending something doesn't exist, perhaps the problem will go away.

Male jealousy of offspring is quite a common problem, and is also dealt with on page 120. It is often difficult to diagnose jealousy, because it may appear as indifference, or as an exaggerated show of "independent" behaviour. Jealousy presupposes vulnerability and dependence, and these are not characteristics that many men feel comfortable to acknowledge as part of their make-up.

A woman whose husband withdraws should ask herself whether she is making him feel needed and wanted. It may be that in her anxiety to look after the baby, she has shut him out and made him feel superfluous. It's a vicious circle. The less he helps, the more responsibility she has; the more she "fusses" around the baby, the more rejected he feels.

One woman eventually broke down under the pressure, and at last her partner understood how much she needed him:

"Unbelievable sense of responsibility. Partner very selfish – went out to golf etc. – I felt totally alone and weepy. After crying outburst, my partner marvellous."

Exhaustion and responsibility

A lot of women felt quite crushed for a time under the weight of hard, physical work and emotional responsibility that had landed on them. As one woman put it:

"A woman is supposed to go through childbirth then come home and carry on almost as normal, even though she is exhausted, leaking everywhere, suffering from depression and feeling as if she has been run over by a steamroller. It gets easier after about six months."

It is important to remember that last sentence: it really does get easier. But in the meantime, looking after a newborn infant is not exactly a piece of cake.

"I felt overwhelmed with exhaustion and terrified when the reality of being responsible for such a young dependent human being hit me."

"After our ignorant bliss, reality set in. It wasn't a pleasant time. I felt rotten after the Caesarean and the baby screamed all day. My husband tried his best to help in all ways, but his job was demanding and he needed to work harder and longer to make more money. We both felt desperate and I felt extremely alone – though I knew he was trying, I felt I had got the raw end of the deal."

"All I remember now is getting my husband's meals at odd times (he worked shifts), while trying to feed a baby that did not want to feed, cried a lot and only slept one or two hours a night."

"Difficulty in lifting due to [Caesarean] operation and muscle separation caused by carrying a large (9lb) baby during pregnancy; tiredness; swollen ankles for six days. We mainly ate takeaway or ready-made meals for the first two or three weeks, until I could move and organize myself better."

Take-away and ready-made meals are a good idea when you're under pressure, and until you can work out a manageable routine. Some things have to go, and housework should be one of them. Just concentrate on the basics, and don't blame yourself for neglecting the rest.

"This baby didn't fill me with immediate love"

The process of bonding starts at birth, when the baby is laid straight on his mother's chest, and the parents are left alone to cuddle him and start to get to know his little body. But bonding doesn't always happen immediately, particularly if the hospital's routine testing intervenes and separates the family at this important early stage.

Some mothers worry that this will have a lasting effect on their relationship with their baby, but as bonding is a gradual process, you will have plenty of time to get close. In some cases, particularly when the parents are under stress from other directions, it can take a few months before you feel the growth of a true rapport. Mothers often feel guilty and unnatural if they don't love their babies straight away, and if this has happened to you, it may be some comfort to read the accounts that follow, which will show that you aren't alone.

"Could not accept the responsibility. Resented the baby and the ties it made on me, resented the time and effort needed to look after it. I never felt like a family. I divorced the baby from us. I was too young and immature."

"I thought I had given birth to a monster. He did nothing by the book, turned night into day and cried almost constantly. I felt drained and disappointed."

"I can't think of any real pleasures, because it seemed to both of us to be wet nappies, sick, and a screaming child that for the first 20 months of his life slept two hours out of 24. We lived in Berlin so there was no family around to give advice and help. Our son was six months old before I even liked him."

"I felt depressed at my weight and permanently tired out, even though I know he was a good baby. I don't feel I really bonded at birth with him, it was all such a shock to my system. I didn't like the feeling of responsibility, a baby needing me. I was happy to leave him with his dad. Luckily, his dad seemed very close to him."

"My baby didn't sleep well and I felt exhausted. I described my feelings for the baby as a love-hate relationship. I found the 24-hour, 7-days-a-week responsibility overwhelming, and didn't feel my husband shared the responsibility."

And one woman courageously describes how she came close to harming her baby:

"I was quite tired as we were living abroad and had no family there to help. I loved being close to the baby, breastfeeding and watching her grow. My partner went out more and more and when the baby cried I felt helpless, isolated and very angry. Because I was alone so much in the evenings it took enormous self-control not to harm the baby. I know now that I didn't understand why she cried. I believed she could help it and did it deliberately to exhaust me!"

"I felt alone and inadequate"

Looking back on the first weeks of their babies' lives, some women remember a feeling of hopeless inadequacy. Two of the women who felt helpless were nurses, and therefore all the more disappointed at "letting themselves down".

"Firstly, I hadn't a clue what to do with my new baby. He had colic after two weeks and that didn't go until he was seven weeks. My mum and mum-in-law came nearly every day to help out. Couldn't have managed without them."

"Even though a nursery nurse, I felt totally inadequate and unprepared for motherhood. I was constantly consulting a baby book for reassurance."

"Anxious, and I felt I was being watched and that I should be able to cope as I am a nursery nurse. However, I still had all the anxieties every new mum feels, and I felt scared to kiss and cuddle my new son until it sunk in that he was mine and he wasn't going home to anyone else at the end of the day."

"My husband couldn't have time off work, my mother had to come and stay for the first week, I had very painful stitches, my daughter cried constantly, we were both very tired. My husband was very patient with both of us, but the first six weeks were hell. I felt quite useless and incapable – not a situation I was used to."

One man puts into words some of the worries a new parent feels at what seem like quite simple tasks:

"Afraid the bath water too hot. Nappy changing at first was not too successful. Often found motions going down one leg."

Fortunately, parents usually become expert at bathing and changing their babies quite quickly.

Post-natal depression

Just after the tremendous physical and emotional experience of giving birth, when your body is undergoing quite dramatic hormonal changes, it is natural to experience both tumultuous happiness and what seems like grief at the same time. You have, after all, "lost" from your body a living being that was very close to you, and your body without it can seem very empty and devoid of purpose.

A minority of women in this survey — probably about one in ten — suffered quite badly from depression during the first months of their babies' lives. Reading some of their accounts below, it is clear that depression stems from a feeling of inadequacy. The mothers who were really depressed felt they could not cope with looking after their babies, and sometimes they couldn't even relate to them. Their relationship with their husbands deteriorated. Unless you have a partner who can understand what is happening to you, and offer emotional and practical support, this can be a dangerous time for a marriage. It is interesting that several of the women who suffered the most were nurses, who could not live up to the high standards they had set themselves.

Depression lifts when you start to take control and realize your own power and your own natural ability. It helps if you stop demanding perfection from yourself and just take things as they come. Then you will start to enjoy your baby rather than seeing looking after her as an insuperable challenge.

The first account comes from a neonatal sister, who was well used to giving other mothers very firm advice.

"I felt very alone and to a great extent quite inadequate. I was at a total loss. I didn't know how to cope. Everything had to be by the book. Suddenly here I was all on my own when I was used to going to work five days a week with a turnover of 100 patients a month. Needless to say, I suffered from post-natal depression. I had a very understanding husband. For weeks he came home from work to find a sobbing wife, the housework not done and the food not prepared. He took me to the family GP and kissed away my tears. He loved his son. Gradually I grew more confident, and then it became a piece of cake. I met other mothers with young children, and when we got together for coffee mornings, all our problems seemed so trivial, but when one is alone, they manifest tenfold.

A lesser volume of love and our marriage would have been demolished in the first few weeks of our son's life. I can remember my husband saying to the GP that I simply was not the woman he married."

"I cried all the time for four months. My husband and I had no relationship. I was ready to go crazy and hated the child."

"Depression. My husband could not understand my needs and I felt very lonely. I loved my baby very much although her crying moods affected me. My mother helped a lot as mothers do, but I really needed some more support from my husband, as we had both shared in the baby's creation."

"I was very ill and developed post-natal depression. I was completely exhausted. I was completely unprepared for the amount of work and the lack of sleep. Everyone expected me to be so happy and I wasn't."

"The main problem was tiredness and weakness after the [Caesarean] operation. Also tearfulness with post-natal depression. I remember thinking it was all a ghastly mistake. My daughter also never slept more than a few hours at a time, day or night. She finally slept through the night when she was four years old."

"I suffered quite severe post-natal depression [after an emergency Caesarean]. I felt my life was not my own – the baby had taken over completely and demanded constant attention."

"After the birth of my second child I had a hormone problem that caused mood swings. Because the baby was 10 days overdue … I retained some of the placenta, which my blood supply was still feeding for another month; my body thought I was pregnant for 10½ months, and that took a bit of getting over. Sometimes I could tackle anything and be a super mum, but sometimes I couldn't even be bothered to open the curtains all day. Then all I could focus on was the children. They were fed, changed and bathed, but no one else was. I never took pills for these mood swings, and eventually sussed out that a good long walk with the children got me out of the house, helped me meet people and talk to them and made me feel that I had done something. I got over all that after two years."

"I didn't bond with the baby for the first six weeks and to compensate I cuddled him all the time. I felt terrified I was not being a good mother and wouldn't let my partner do anything in case he saw how inadequate I was. The baby didn't sleep; I was tired and depressed. We had recently moved, my partner had started a new job and worked long hours to prove himself. I had no friends, both parents were dead and my in-laws were 200 miles away. I had no support. Looking back, it's no wonder I was so depressed. At the time I just thought I was inadequate, so strove even harder to be the perfect wife and mother. I'm amazed the marriage survived."

This last account shows how important it is not to create additional difficulties for yourself around the time of childbirth. It is not a good idea for your partner to change jobs, to start travelling long distances to work, or to work away from home. It is not advisable to move just before you have a baby, because you will feel isolated away from friends and family. Think of transport, and think of how you will get to the shops, or out to meet people. Try, if possible, to arrange for some extra help from relatives or friends until you get on top of your situation.

Problems with feeding

Not being able to feed your baby properly causes a great deal of anxiety. The accounts below indicate that this is quite a common problem. Its resolution usually lies with you, the mother, using your instincts. The advice of nurses, midwives, mothers-in-law and husbands all pales into insignificance in the face of your own commonsense. Breastfeed if you want to and if you can; otherwise, don't feel guilty about turning to the bottle.

"My daughter was a difficult feeder – had to be bottle-fed every two hours – shattering for me and worrying."

"I was very keen to do everything 'properly' and was determined to breastfeed. I did so for about six months but I think I should have given up earlier – this was a worrying decision as I felt I'd failed – I was so unsure about her getting enough from me."

"Feeding was a great problem. The baby was very jaundiced and couldn't breastfeed. I was very sore through his trying, and always expressing milk. Once he could breastfeed, he wasn't getting enough, so I had to top him up by bottle. He always came awake wanting to play around 11.35 [p.m.], and feeling so tired myself I had problems settling him. My husband was not supportive at all. He felt he had to work during the day, so wasn't prepared to get himself up to help during the night, or to take turns."

"She didn't sleep well. She seemed to have colic and was always crying until late at night, and was always sick after her feeds. I breastfed and she took ages to feed. I was up during the night a couple of times, and although we loved having her, I began to get very tired."

"When I brought my son home from hospital, he suddenly went on to two-hourly feeding. For the first week or so, I seemed to be feeding and changing and had no time for anything else. I was horrified, as I'd had no idea I would be so tied. My husband had to get all the meals, otherwise we'd never have eaten. I struggled to breastfeed for several weeks, but never produced an adequate supply and he had dreadful colic. However, I'm sad to say (because I felt a failure) that he thrived on the bottle and settled down well."

149

"The baby was beautiful and I was awestricken holding her, thinking to myself: Is she mine? Feeding her wasn't exactly easy. The nurse who tried to teach me how was terribly forceful and made me feel very stressed. In the end when I was home I had to bottle-feed her."

"Too much to do. Unprepared for the feeding demands and washing etc. Breastfeeding a problem as there were teenage stepsons at home and I felt selfconscious so spent a lot of time with the baby alone upstairs. This made my husband feel shut out."

Finally, one woman stresses how important it is for both partners to know exactly what happens to a woman's body during pregnancy and childbirth. Her ex-husband refused to go to ante-natal classes, but she didn't realize the depths of his ignorance.

"My ex thought an operation was needed so that I could breastfeed. Until he admitted he didn't know how the milk got out, we had terrible rows. I wanted to breastfeed, but he didn't want me to. The reason, it turned out, was that he didn't want me to have the operation that made holes! This was in 1981."

 Did you stay at home to look after your baby? How did you cope with loss of independence?

Most women in the survey stayed home initially, but few gave up work completely. Some went back to work as soon as they could, for financial reasons and because they missed the stimulation of a job and adult company; many waited until their youngest child was at school.

Some loved the opportunity to devote themselves to rearing a family, and those who enjoyed it most say that looking after their baby meant that they gained independence and responsibility, not lost it.

"I stayed at home but never felt the loss of independence. To me, looking after my baby and shaping a new life was the most rewarding job anyone could do. My husband was happy to provide and never made us seem like a burden."

"I hadn't lost my independence, I'd gained a new and important responsibility."

"I did not lose independence – I gained it. I could choose when to work and what to do. I made friends at the mother and baby group which I have kept to this day. My days are full and happy."

"I realized my true vocation! After the awful first months I loved motherhood, being able to spend more time out of doors and not having a nine-to-five job."

Two women describe how badly they missed their babies when lack of money forced them back to work before they were emotionally ready for it:

"I returned to work when the baby was seven weeks old. I missed my baby terribly – my mother and a friend shared the childminding. With the second baby I gave up work completely and enjoyed the freedom. I found it difficult not having any money of my own and have since returned to work, but overall I loved being at home."

"I stayed at home for six months – great! I hated my job anyway, but then I had to go back. I was angry at my husband for forcing me back to work. I cried every day, but that could have been because I didn't totally trust my childminder. She used to give him sweets and not use the proper baby seat in the car. After six months I gave in my notice to look after him myself. I have never felt that I have lost my independence because I have always considered my role as a parent to be ultimately important, though the loss of my wages remains a severe blow."

This last woman eventually solved her problems by becoming a registered childminder herself, and taking an evening job in a bar. Several other women in the survey also became childminders, getting qualified by taking a course of evening classes, and one also took up part-time dressmaking.

Sadly, very few employers in this country as yet provide creches, and only one woman reports that she was able to find a part-time job to which she could take her baby.

Other women were less concerned with making ends meet than with keeping in touch with the world outside their own four walls. Through mother-and-toddler groups and other organizations, a baby can provide you with a connection to potential new friends:

"Kept in touch with old friends and made new ones through the baby. Taught myself new skills in homemaking to make the money go further. *Sometimes* felt depressed."

151

"I coped by joining NCT [National Childbirth Trust] and becoming involved socially, leaving my husband to babysit. I went to evening classes and social activities that I felt were 'for me'."

One woman gave herself a break by putting her little son in a nursery for just one day a week, "to ensure I don't lose myself". Another pursued former interests in the evenings while her husband looked after the baby:

"My husband and I both sat on a number of committees, and we babysat for each other so that we could go out some evenings. It was more important for me to meet other people than him, so I didn't feel isolated. Until my son was able to stand, I found it almost impossible to go to the nearest town on the bus, as I couldn't hold him and put the buggy up and down. It was the only time when I felt really tied."

Two women acknowledge that staying at home was not easy for them, but are glad that they stuck at it:

"I was so taken up with my new baby that I really don't think I saw it as a loss of independence. Even now after six years of childrearing I would not say that I've lost my independence. I do get hacked off sometimes because of the sheer bloody hard work that young children involve, but because I've got no family near me this has in some ways made me quite resourceful and organized. My husband has always been supportive to me emotionally and practically with the children, even though he works long hours and is often away for a week or two at a time. He has never been dismissive of my role in the family/relationship, and we've got lots of respect for each other and for our roles."

"It was difficult staying home at first, but I kept telling myself that it was worth the sacrifice to see my daughters growing up. I never regretted it – the time goes so quickly!"

But for others, the difficulties seem to have outweighed the pleasures and rewards. Loneliness can be a big problem. When you leave behind a satisfying job and colleagues whose company you enjoy, to devote yourself full-time to a demanding baby, there is a big adjustment to make and adult company is often sorely missed.

"I stayed at home and found it very lonely. It was all new and I didn't really have a routine (which I needed). After working full-time it was totally different and very hard to adjust."

"My parents are dead. My husband's parents did not help at all. I felt trapped with a continually crying baby in a town where I knew nobody. Above all, I missed the adult conversation from work and everything about going out, earning money, meeting people – my own life."

"My husband had changed job and we had only lived in our new home for a year. I didn't know many people, the locals were very stand-offish, so I did feel very lonely."

"It was more the camaraderie that I missed than the loss of independence."

"I stayed at home and felt this was the right thing to do. But it took me a long time to adjust to losing my independence and I became lonely and bored."

"It was very difficult, as my partner was working away. I was lonely and wanted more help."

In a number of cases, the feeling of being left out of the mainstream of life was exacerbated by having a partner whose life had changed hardly at all, and who went on as normal with his career and his social life uninterrupted by the arrival of the infant. For some women, the balance between themselves and their partner was destroyed, and they began to harbour a dangerous resentment.

"I stayed home. I resented the fact that he still took off when it suited him – though the newness and novelty were worth it."

"Stayed at home until daughter 10 months. Missed independence terribly. Found it hard not to have anyone to talk to. Lonely. No family at all in area. Felt resentful."

"Felt bored, depressed. Resented my husband having a life outside home."

"I felt I'd lost a lot of my identity as an individual and that my brain was stagnating. I was a bore and had to get back to work. I was irritable and short-tempered. I resented the fact that I was stuck in the house so much and took it out on my husband."

"I did not cope with loss of independence very well. I felt isolated after six months when the thrill and excitement wore off. None of my good friends was pregnant – they were all still at work. I became very resentful of my husband. We began slowly to grow apart."

"I felt totally confined to the house as we moved just before the birth and I had no friends or outside contacts. My husband was very busy at work so I felt very neglected."

These women are only one step away from feeling a loss of identity. If the blame for the wipe-out of your individuality falls on your partner, as it's almost bound to do, it can cripple your marriage. The women below felt totally crushed.

"Yes, I did stay at home and I felt without my identity."

"I allowed my dwindling individuality to totally fizzle out."

"There are times when I would like to go out and be a person again, not just a mum."

"I'm still at home and have not been apart from the baby since she was born. I'm still feeling angry with myself for losing my independence."

Some women felt their loss of independence most acutely in their purses. Even when working partners are very generous, it is very difficult sometimes to treat their money as your own and to spend it on personal things like clothes. For several women, the crunch came when they had to ask for money to buy their husband's Christmas presents. The only solution was to go back to work.

"After the first three months of paid leave I took three months of unpaid leave. This was totally demoralizing. I even had to ask my husband for money to buy his own Christmas present. After six months I went back to work for two days a week. It was nice to be my own person again."

"Yes. It was hard – felt strange spending 'his' money – especially birthdays and Christmas."

"I don't like having to ask for money for things like presents for my husband and for clothes for me."

"To begin with, I stayed at home, but went back to work as soon as possible because I couldn't stand the loss of financial independence."

"I stayed at home for two years, then went out to start my own business. I hated the loss of independence, as my husband was very selfish with his money."

"I got a part-time job when the baby was six months old. I didn't want to, but we needed the money. On top of this, I hated having no income of my own (after having worked since leaving school), and absolutely detested having to ask my partner for money. It wasn't that he made it awkward or anything – it just made me feel that I was nothing, having to ask for money. I hated being away from my daughter when I was at work too."

Only two couples in this survey tried completely reversing the traditional roles. The first is a woman with a high-powered career, whose husband was 62 when their baby was born.

"I went back to work when my son was six weeks old. I cried – I hated leaving him, but my husband stayed home to look after him, relieved by my mother and sister-in-law. He did a very good job, so after a few weeks I relaxed, but felt guilty."

The second is a man who was forced out of work by ill-health.

"I suffered a stroke when the baby was 18 months old. My wife, who fortunately had trained as a nurse, had junior and me to cope with, but when I was back on my feet but couldn't work, she went out and did odd waitressing jobs in hotels part-time. We reversed roles, so perhaps it wasn't as bad for my wife as it is for some. No doubt I created more problems because I took my frustrations out on the family, but I wasn't conscious of it at the time."

It would be interesting to know more about the frustrations he suffered. If you can reverse roles, even for just a short while, it is bound to give the working partner a better understanding of the demands and restrictions on the life of the one who stays at home.

Though staying at home to look after your baby can be the most fulfilling time of your life, it doesn't suit everyone. It is very important to have adequate support from your partner, to have relatives or friends you can spend time with during the day, and to keep up old interests and find new ones.

If you are one of the many mothers who feel they have lost out by giving up their jobs, financial independence and workmates, you need to beware against resentment building up towards your partner that could harm your relationship and sour the atmosphere in your home, which will inevitably affect your child.

Don't allow yourself to be a victim: take responsibility for your own wellbeing and get back into the swing of things. Get more help from your partner to give you time to yourself, take a part-time job, perhaps working at home as a childminder, or consider leaving your baby with someone you trust so that you can return to work full-time.

Q: Did you neglect your partner? Was he jealous?

When a mother gives up her old lifestyle to stay at home and look after a new baby, as most women in this survey did, at least for a while, her partner can feel as though he's been demoted to number two position in her attention and affections. If he reacts by spending more time away from home, their lives begin to diverge and the relationship deteriorates.

Some couples understood that this situation would be only temporary, and put up with it, knowing that the closeness would return.

"After the second baby [in 18 months] I just hadn't enough time for my partner and we both felt we were losing the closeness we once had, but we recognized that in time the demands of the two children would lessen. If we had been younger and less mature, our relationship might have deteriorated at this point, as it had in my husband's first marriage."

As the woman above indicates, this can be a dangerous time for a relationship. The next contributor had a calmer and more long-sighted approach, and put her partner first:

"I remember having a deep intuitive feeling, after the birth of our third son, that I did not own the children, that they were their own people. My job as a mother was to bring them up in the best way that I knew how and to encourage their own individual talents and confidence so that, when they felt ready to leave home, they were emotionally and practically equipped to lead independent lives. Also, once the children had gone, I was going to be left with my husband and if I didn't put that relationship before the relationship with my children, I was going to be left with nothing."

And the next woman, who has a very happy marriage, has continued to put her husband first:

"Somehow we realized that we were both paying more attention to the baby than to each other. We decided to set aside some time each day for us, when baby was out of the way in bed. We did what we wanted then – watched TV or talked (babies taboo). Sometimes 10 minutes was all we had, in bed before going to sleep, but we had our time, some time, every day. These days we have our Saturday nights. The kids are banished to the playroom at 7pm. At 8.00 we go and say it's bedtime, and that's that. They understand. We have a takeaway meal, talk or watch TV. It's like being single again, because we know the kids won't disturb us, because it's Saturday night! We have explained to them that they have their special things to do where parents are excluded – after-school activities, ballet and so on – and we have our Saturday nights. They think it's fair, so it works."

The couples who survived the hard work and the refocussing of attention most successfully – and enjoyed it – were those who put the most energy into sharing parenthood.

"My partner took an active part in baby care. He was not jealous."

"As we both loved her, no problems."

"No. I tried to include my husband in the baby's needs; in fact he became very efficient at nappy changing and bottle feeding. We agreed right from the beginning it would be 'our' baby and we would make a 'joint effort' in looking after our children whenever possible."

"He's never been jealous. I was happy to hand over the baby to him when he got in from work for him to play with and feed while I cooked dinner."

"No! I used to like to sit close to him while feeding the baby and talk or hold hands."

"No. We were both very conscious of the importance of giving time to each other, and my husband shared our baby at every opportunity."

And two men write:

"Baby was shared. I always had a baby hour, either bathing babies or putting them in their cots."

"My wife feels she did neglect me – meals were hurried, talked about the children, tired. Little time alone together. I did not feel neglected or jealous, even though the first child was a poor sleeper. I liked being a dad."

Where there was no sharing there was a problem. Sometimes an over-anxious mother can shut out her partner because she feels he is unqualified to deal with the baby as well as she does. One woman describes how she learned from her mistakes:

"I was so wrapped up in caring for our daughter, making sure everyone crept around silently when she was asleep, and I was so fussy about everything that although I didn't think I was neglecting him, I now realize I was. He definitely felt neglected and it wasn't until we sat down together to iron out a few problems that he admitted he was deliberately staying behind late at work because he didn't want to come home. (There was no one else involved.) The second time things were much smoother and I made an effort not to exclude him."

Men who feel excluded react in different ways. One felt totally at sea:

"He felt helpless and useless and wondered if we had done the right thing in starting a family at all."

Many women long for partners who involve themselves more, but the following two persisted in keeping their husbands at bay, perhaps because they felt unsure of their own abilities as carers for their babies:

"He was jealous, but because he wanted the chance to look after the baby more."

"He may have felt emotionally supplanted by the baby, explaining his over-involvement in every aspect of baby care."

Other men who felt pushed out expressed their hurt feelings by making sexual demands that could not be willingly accommodated. One man was proprietorially resentful when he saw the baby suckling his partner's breasts.

"Because of broken nights, I was usually too tired to enjoy sex, although my husband often insisted! I also used to neglect the housework sometimes, which made him resentful. He admitted to jealousy of the baby at times."

"He really had very little to do with the baby, only when it was bathed and ready for bed. He did feel neglected, as I was always tired when he arrived home and never really did much to myself, or look sexy enough for him, which he frequently said."

"I felt he was unreasonable. He gave no help at all. Nor did he allow me to recover before resuming sex."

"He expected everything to be as before, with the dinner on the table, house tidied etc., and hated my breastfeeding as he felt it was his body the baby had taken."

There may be quite a fine line between feeling excluded from the completeness of the union between mother and baby and actually being given the cold shoulder, but some men didn't hang around long enough to find out what they felt. Completely unsuited for the emotional responsibility of fatherhood, which other men see as an adventure that stretches their experience and deepens their love, these men reverted to a bachelor lifestyle.

"He reverted to the same routine he'd had before marriage. Home from office, tea, straight out to pub."

"Yes, I probably did neglect him. After my second pregnancy he was not around much anyway. I did not want to see him particularly."

"I don't think he felt neglected, partly because he was never there."

"Yes, I think I did neglect my partner, but purposely, as I felt he was neglecting me and our family by not spending any time with us, and when he did he was either drunk or hungover."

"I did not neglect my husband as he was not around to neglect."

Interestingly, a handful of women said that they, and not their partners, were the ones who felt jealous and neglected. One was jealous of all the attention her baby had from friends and relatives. Another needed constant reassurance from her husband that he still loved her. Two replies show that a feeling of inadequacy lies at the root of this jealousy:

"For the first few months I was very depressed and was unable to breastfeed, so my husband did a lot of the caring. He and our son became very close. He felt more worried about me."

"No. *I* got jealous when he succeeded in getting her off to sleep and I couldn't."

These answers underline the importance of partners taking joint charge of babycare. Only by handling your baby yourself can you start to learn about her and become adept at looking after her. Love for the child grows out of this knowledge and closeness. Without practice, it is easy to feel inadequate as a parent, and to withdraw. Jealousy and feelings of exclusion can be avoided if you decide in advance that you want to share looking after your children. Without sharing, it's:

". . . a vicious circle. Baby demands – you're tired – he's jealous – feeds, nappies – non-stop."

Q: How did you feel about being a family?

About two thirds felt very positive about family life. Many of the answers mention a sense of togetherness and belonging, a cosy feeling, a feeling of completeness, and deepening love for their partner that grew over the years. A sense of growth is evident in the answers that follow:

"I felt much more complete, particularly after our second child. I was more confident and relaxed about family life. I believe my husband and I felt closer because of our family."

"We loved being a family straight away. I'd doubled the amount of people I loved and the amount of people my husband loved. The main change in my feeling towards my husband was that I relied on him."

"Parenthood added an extra dimension to our marriage. Our son added an extra dimension of fun."

"We are very happy being a family and wouldn't have been as happy as this childless. We do childish things with the kids that without them we wouldn't do (playing at swings, footballing on the field, sledging in the snow).

We'd look daft building sandcastles on our own, wouldn't we? Having kids allows us to do these things with them, brings helpless fits of laughter, and brings us all closer together. We know more about each other since we've had the kids. It's made us talk about our own childhoods and deepened the love and the bond."

One man writes that though he had been worried about the responsibility of being a father, he discovered he enjoyed it. Another says:

"I think we got closer. I think being a family and being part of a family makes us stronger and more able to cope with the problems that beset us."

Some of the warmest answers come from women who in watching their partners develop as fathers have discovered new reasons for loving them.

"Sometimes I have to pinch myself – when I think I have a husband and children I bubble up inside with all sorts of happy emotions. I grew to love my partner very very much, more than I can put into words."

"After the first few weeks I began to feel being a family was quite normal and I couldn't remember previously. My love for my husband intensified as he was just brilliant at being a dad."

"I enjoyed seeing my husband develop as a father."

"It was lovely being a family. My feelings didn't change, except for loving him more, as I saw what a loving, caring, tender father he had become."

"A sense of completeness, a positive force. I discovered different sides to my partner, enriched my love for him, also my maternal feelings enveloped him."

"We love being a family. My older one loves the sense of belonging. I love and respect my husband much more for being a good father."

"We thoroughly enjoy going out as a family and doing things together. I felt more loving towards him for producing a lovely baby."

And one man describes how parenthood enabled his relationship to grow:

"I felt proud, contented, needed, happy. My wife became reliant on me emotionally, financially, more than before. It made her realize she needed me. I had always needed my wife – she's my best friend, but seeing her as a mother really made me stand back and admire the woman I'd married and the way she coped with everything."

Of those who had a bad experience of family life, most were women who complained of their partner's lack of involvement. In some cases, mothers put up with looking after the family single-handed, even though they resented it, but in others, this was the beginning of the end of the relationship.

"I felt as though I was single-handedly running the whole show and I *hated* my partner for putting so much on me. I had little respect for him."

"We weren't a family. He worked more, socialized alone, refused to go on holiday, was never home to share meals or any family time, and I resented his lack of support, interest and involvement."

"I began to resent the fact, and still do, that I have always got up in the night for our two children when they were babies or if they were ill. If I asked my husband to help, he would be very reluctant to disturb his sleep, moaning that if he didn't have his sleep, he wouldn't be able to work the next day."

"My husband had to spend more time at work. He was also in the TA [Territorial Army], which meant he was away most weekends, so I began to feel that as he was never there as a father or husband he might as well leave."

"I found my husband supportive to an extent, then it was 'on your own, kiddo'. Unfortunately, I began to question many things in our relationship."

"I felt we weren't a family as I seemed to be bringing up my son on my own. I wanted support or a little help, but the more I said about it, the more hours he seemed to work."

"Husband always in pub. Didn't feel I had a family. Hostile slightly."

In some cases, women focussed all their attention on their new babies, excluding their partners and ceasing to see them as sexual beings. Not surprisingly, the relationship suffered.

"The responsibility scared me, but I had no qualms about putting aside time and personal interests for my children. My interests have changed, and I now see my partner more as a provider and companion than a fun-loving sexual partner."

"I felt more complete and settled as a mother [had waited two years to become pregnant]. I was too impatient and expected him to understand why I was very mumsy and stop-at-home, not mistressy, as before."

"I loved being a family. But I felt superior to my husband because he couldn't cope with a baby. I found it harder to love him."

"I loved my baby more than I could imagine and focussed all my attention on him. I stopped seeing my partner and myself as sexual beings, and I blamed him for my depression and feeling of being trapped."

And some women who could not take responsibility let the situation get on top of them and felt that they just were not cut out for motherhood.

"I felt cheated. Nobody had explained about the pressures of parenthood. I drifted away from my husband."

"Overwhelming responsibility. We just existed together."

"I found myself resenting how much effort I had to put into everything for others."

"On becoming a mother I lost my individuality completely."

"All our decisions revolved around the baby and baby gear whenever we went anywhere. I felt increasingly bitter that only *my* life had been altered."

"I felt disappointed, a drudge who couldn't control the house, the baby or the situation – mainly through lack of sleep and loneliness."

Perhaps the writers above would sympathize with the woman who realized she hadn't really wanted children in the first place:

"Felt OK, but I would say that social pressure was very great at that time to produce children – regarded as odd if you didn't. Wished partner would help more."

Finally, three women tell of their experience of adding to their existing families with the child of a new partner. The first married a man nine years her junior. She already had three children by her first husband, who didn't pay maintenance. She got pregnant accidentally by her new partner and worried that the whole experience would prove too much ot a responsibility for him. It worked out, despite his anxiety over how to earn enough money to support them all:

"I was very happy about being a family, and my feelings towards my husband heightened, for his guts in taking us all on. Just about everything was shared, apart from feeding, as I breastfed."

Another couple had five children from previous marriages:

"Our other children loved the new baby, but I think I suffered from a bit of post-natal depression, as I often had temper tantrums and weeping sessions, mainly because of my husband's seeming indifference to me. He admits now that he was so worried about coping financially that he shut himself off from me. But as time went on he became a marvellous father to all six children."

And the third couple already had two children between them:

"Having the new baby was lovely for us all, not just my husband and myself. It made the whole family closer."

These answers provide a simple guideline: if you both want to be actively involved in parenthood, the chances are that it will be an immeasurably rewarding experience that will deepen your love for each other. If your partner doesn't understand and look forward to the responsibility he will be taking on, the risk is that you'll be running the home and family single-handed. If you want to safeguard your relationship, talk out your reservations before you get pregnant. Try to isolate and examine outside pressures to have children from your family, friends, and society at large.

 How has parenthood changed your relationship?

The most positive answers come from couples who have worked together to bring up their children. Sharing in the daily routine brings a closeness and a satisfaction not felt by couples who carefully delineate their roles. The couples who are getting the most out of their marriages have found a natural balance in their lives: they work as a team at being parents, but put each other first. They are alive to each other as individuals, still learning and developing, singly as well as together. Parenthood has added a new and fulfilling dimension to their relationship, and brings a sense of permanence that is relaxing and confidence-inspiring. Love mellows and deepens.

"It has mellowed and changed in ways that are sometimes surprisingly beneficial. We have grown used to compromise. We have overcome many family crises together, and the relief from resolving these has brought us closer."

"It is stronger, we are closer, we have shared everything together, although some times have been very difficult for us (we have a six-year-old hyperactive child), but because we are honest and open with one another and believe in ourselves and in each other, our relationship survives. We are best friends as well as husband and wife."

"It has been through many stages. We now work as a team together with the children. We know each other so well now. Arguments no longer last more than a few minutes. We comfort each other when the children get us down."

"We have come a long way from being a couple of lustful teenagers just enjoying each other's company with no commitment, to being parents. Our relationship has matured, developed and deepened. We often have the same thoughts and like the same things. We can easily step in to take over what the other is doing. My husband was once unemployed for two weeks. During this time I had the chance to work extra hours, so we completely swapped roles. It made him realize what exactly is involved with running a home, organizing children, shopping, cooking etc. Now he realizes what has to be done without my having to ask."

"Our relationship has just kept getting better. We've had our ups and downs, especially after the birth of each baby, and with my husband's job, but I'd much rather have the relationship we've got today than that when we first married, although at the time I didn't think there was anything wrong with it. Today our relationship is still growing and changing and it's quite exciting to be in the process of rediscovering each other again now that our daughter is 10 months old."

"We are closer now than ever because we are able to talk to each other. We make sure the children are in bed early so we can have time together as ourselves and not just as mummy and daddy. We also manage to get the occasional weekend away without the children. We look on each other as friends, lovers and confidantes as well as spouses."

165

"Mellowed. We are more tolerant of each other's needs. We argue rarely, whereas we argued a lot in the early stages of our marriage [before the baby]. We are definitely more compatible. We have tried to keep up our individual interests, yet do a lot together as a family too. My husband has taken on more responsibility for organizing our lives with regard to running the finances, paperwork etc."

"We continue to pursue our different interests and maybe it's keeping our own independence that has helped us keep the glow of affection burning. We are both looking forward to when the children are grown up and we can spend time alone together again and rekindle the love of just two and not four. The children have certainly moulded us two together. It sealed us."

Couples who are happy together describe each other as best friends, and more tolerant, affectionate, understanding, flexible, caring and mature. They say they are less selfish and argumentative, and miss each other a lot when they're apart.

"More settled. We row rarely. We have become more open, patient, and forgiving."

"It has grown from a friendly relationship to a loving, caring, trusting one. Also we seem to need each other, not just sexually."

"Our love is much deeper because we have experienced pain and joy together and have always been there to support one another."

"It has grown. We have confidence in each other, trust each other and are friends as well as lovers."

"Initial feelings of physical attraction developed into a true friendship. You learn to cope with each other's moods and emotional problems better as time goes on."

"We have become more considerate of each other's feelings. We know each other's thoughts, almost."

"We have both matured. Although my husband has always been considerate, he can now see what needs to be done without being asked. He is totally involved with childcare as I have had to return to work. I have been a lot more relaxed about everything since our second child."

"We are both more patient and easygoing. My husband is more mature and sensitive. But we're both the same as we were before, as well."

"I felt more secure and faithful – loved partner more than before. He felt the same. More attentive and caring."

Several people gained strengths that amazed them:

"I changed emotionally from a pacifist to a mother tiger – although I still hold pacifist views! Just let nobody test them out by threatening my children! I wasn't prepared for the intensity of the protectiveness I feel. When I imagine someone threatening to harm my children, I find my violent emotions alarming!"

"My wife stopped worrying about unimportant things, became more confident in public, more assertive, e.g. she started requesting feeding/changing rooms in stores, challenging doctors' opinions. I became more mature and responsible, yet retained a sense of humour. But in the early days I did worry over little things."

Hard work, but worth it

Some have reached a satisfying level of togetherness and understanding after weathering very rocky patches during the early years of their relationship.

"The early years were difficult, but as time went by we began to piece together a new lifestyle. I felt we had to get to know each other all over again. Patience and understanding were in great demand and a new kind of love was born."

"We have a very strong relationship – our early years were a struggle emotionally and financially. We never considered separating – it was not an issue. We loved the baby too much and knew this was a change in life to be dealt with. You have to fight and not give in. Of course love flies out of the window, but ride the storm and it returns again eventually. We learned the hard way. But we've just celebrated ten years!

We are different people now. But for the better in some ways. We are unselfish and do everything for the children (we hope). We have kerbed our aspirations and live for the moment. We are not so intense. Our love is divided between our children and each other. We feel complete – not perfection – there's plenty of room for that! But things aren't bad between us and the security is still there."

"We have had a few rocky patches. We have stuck together. It is not easy, but divorce seems a poor alternative!"

"There was a twilight period when things just went from day to day and year to year. But now [age 51] we have developed into very good friends, with no secrets and more loving than ever."

"We decided to part twice, but didn't. I would say that the children have changed our relationship for the better and very dramatically. If it weren't for them we wouldn't still be together. We fight less, for their sake. We have found that we now have less reason to fight."

"We have both learned a lot from our previous mistakes, we know each other *a lot* better and so understand each other – we are very easy with each other and get on with our own hobbies and interests without interfering or throwing tantrums."

"During the first few years we were close. When the children reached toddler/playgroup stage I became heavily involved in the administration of these groups. The phone didn't stop ringing, it became all-consuming and my partner was pushed into the background. We started to lead fairly separate lives.

When the children started school I began to resent my loss of independence and identity. I became just a wife and mother – my personality completely submerged under these roles. When I was 38 I began to fear that the marriage would break up. (I thought history might repeat itself as my parents had split up when I was 12.) We received counselling, and while overall it wasn't that helpful, it did put things back into perspective and encouraged each of us to find ways of making each other feel special again. I returned to work for a few days each week, which helped boost my confidence and independence.

Currently our relationship is much improved, we communicate with each other more effectively, we make the effort to be more caring and sensitive to each other's needs. I believe my partner is coming to terms with my need to be more independent and my own person."

Too much responsibility

For some couples, there is more stress than enjoyment in raising a family, and their relationship sinks under the weight of it. One or two women in the survey admitted that they had made the wrong decision in starting a family.

"It has deteriorated over the years, as the children take over and leave us very little time for each other. The love is still there, but we both feel resentful and hard done-by."

"Having children did force us apart at times – and I remember many heated quarrels over them. In fact we often say if we had known then what we know now, we wouldn't have bothered having children."

"We were a happy-go-lucky carefree rather rebellious couple, though we argued furiously even then. Now we are overburdened, stressed, fed-up and disinterested in each other, and still arguing!"

Answers to another question in the survey (page 182) show that, for most couples, the issue of child discipline causes more arguments than almost any other topic. Young people constantly test themselves against adult authority as part of growing up and learning to be adults themselves, and if parents are not united in their policy of discipline, their children will home in on the difference between them and play one off against the other, causing damaging family rifts. Where parents agree on what is and what isn't allowed, children have a stable framework of guidelines and more security at home.

Finally, here's a woman who definitely isn't cut out for parenthood. She let her children come between herself and her partner, without even managing to be an attentive mother.

"My teenage children ruined my second marriage. They are scheming and crafty and want money all the time – I could tell you stories that would make your hair curl!!! They will either make or break you. My hardest time was when my girls were 14 and 16, and my son 7. They all wanted my *immediate* attention *now* – each thought their exams the most important – so they were – but if you have a partner who wants you to go out for a drink in the evening – what do you do? I lost my partner – he couldn't stand the aggro! Children today are so selfish. I spent 25 years looking after my kids, and the only change I'd make to my life is – I'd never do it again. I got no credit for doing it. Now I'm free and having a ball. Remarried to a lovely man."

Men who seek comfort in an affair

A man who has an affair while his partner is pregnant may believe he needs another woman because he finds pregnancy a turn-off. The deeper truth is more likely to be that he finds pregnancy threatening, because of the real or imagined way in which his partner is forming an exclusive bond with their unborn child. If he feels sexually or emotionally rejected, pushed out of the number one spot in her affections, he may have an affair to give his confidence and self-esteem a necessary boost.

The wife who puts her husband's unfaithfulness down to her own unattractiveness in pregnancy should look more deeply at his motives. The same goes for the woman harrassed by looking after young children who is told by her partner that her clothes are always a mess and she is losing her looks. Behind this superficial and insulting comment lies an unspoken accusation: "You haven't got time for me any more!" Men who find it shaming to admit vulnerability lack the emotional courage to put their need for love and attention into words. They are more likely to express it in action, which often means seeking love and attention from someone else.

This is yet another example of the gap in communication between the sexes. Women can help by anticipating feelings of jealousy and rejection their partners might have, and by not being selfish in their love for their babies, before or after birth. Men can help by opening up and talking about their feelings, remembering that emotional honesty is the quality women most like in men (see pages 24 and 43). Both partners can guard against feelings of exclusion by sharing as much as possible in pregnancy and childcare.

The next contributor's marriage suffered severely during her post-natal depression.

"Apart from a few months of post-natal depression after my second child was born, when my husband felt that I was a totally different person, we have always turned to each other for support. Unfortunately, during the time I was ill, he felt that the world was crumbling around him and I couldn't help, so he turned to someone else. Fortunately, we have been able to put this behind us, apart from the odd occasion, and are even stronger in our relationship than we were before.

A couple of months ago we left the children with their Nan and had a weekend away – our first, and it was great, though we more than once felt like phoning to see if they were OK. We had a wonderful time doing all the things that you can't do with children around. I would certainly recommend a weekend of just being husband and wife rather than mum and dad."

It is quite likely that the husband of the next woman quoted felt safer with his male friends at this time because at least they would not "push him out" to make way for a baby.

"When I was pregnant with our second baby I discovered my husband was bisexual and all physical contact stopped. The relationship was fine until I discovered he had men friends. We stayed together for three years for the sake of the children, but then separated. I am now happily remarried and wish I had children with my second husband, but that isn't possible as I've had a hysterectomy."

Here are four other women with husbands who couldn't cope with their feelings of jealousy and rejection:

"I find it very difficult to be positive about this, but I assume during our early years of parenthood my husband decided it was time to be unfaithful, just like his father before him."

"When I was five months pregnant with our second son, my husband started an affair. It continued for nine months before he confessed. We tried to sort out our feelings for 10 weeks. He says I put too many demands on him to be Mr Perfect (which I thought he was), and he sought solace elsewhere. We are now separated, and both feel it's best for the children."

"When we had the second baby and I had to work in the evening, he wanted his independence from me. I was too tired doing everything and he wanted to have fun all the time. We are legally separated as he went off with someone else."

"My husband [18 years older] drifted away after the birth of our first child. Possibly saw himself free again? He did his own thing after the birth of our second child. He even asked: 'Is this my child?' The third time I got pregnant I had an abortion, but he didn't support me. I've felt guilty ever since. The relationship failed again. At age 50 he went off with another woman. Then he parted from her and from us – he never came back. Now, although we live apart and he is unemployed, so doesn't help financially, we are friends, and go out occasionally. Neither of us has a new partner."

Men who just don't grow up

About two thirds of the people who took part in this survey described marriages that were unsatisfactory in various ways. One of the complaints most commonly voiced by women with children was that their partners made poor fathers. It seems that a great many men are not emotionally mature enough to take on the responsibility of parenthood.

The following answers are typical:

"I started to grow up. He didn't."

"I became more independent and stronger in my opinions on running the house, finances etc. He didn't change at all, carrying on with the bachelor life he led before we met."

"My husband didn't change. He would do things if asked, but never volunteered with the baby or home. I became lonely and depressed, wanting more children once the baby was older. I thought that was the solution to my situation – wrong!"

"We did grow apart in some ways. The baby was my job, and his job was his. I had some help, but not the involvement I'd hoped for."

"I resented the fact that I was tired and he went out so much. I loved him less because very gradually I began to feel that we had little in common. I like to think I became less selfish and gradually as the baby grew I became a good mother. I don't think he changed much and he acted as if he wished he was still a bachelor. He was involved with his job and was probably tired at the end of the day. We didn't communicate very much once we had a second child 2½ years after the first."

"I didn't change, but my partner didn't like the restrictions of having three young children around and he started behaving again like a very young unmarried man."

"He longed for freedom, felt claustrophobic and wanted a 'sophisticated' lifestyle. He talked all the time about his single days in the Navy as being the happiest of his life."

"He spent more time and gave more commitment to the Territorial Army than to me. He spent every weekend away."

"He took up waterskiing and I stayed at home. Money was tight, so couldn't get away for a break. He didn't seem to notice waterskiing is expensive."

"I was left 24 hours with the children while he started going straight from work to pubs and clubs. This lasted for two to three years, then he left."

And in some cases men turn to drink and become violent.

"I was depressed and fat. Him: violence increased, drinking increased. Other women."

"I became more protective towards the baby, angry with my partner. He wouldn't talk about it, drank more, became more violent, more demanding and childish. He used to call me 'mum', and I hated it, and told him so. But he continued, even in public."

All the male behaviour described here, from withdrawal of attention and involvement to physical abuse, is a form of rebellion, a retaliation against the woman for transferring her love to her child. Though some women undoubtedly do exclude their partners quite consciously, others may be unaware that their partners are feeling excluded. It is sometimes difficult to tell, because of course when your partner behaves as though life is far more interesting away from you than with you, whether it's at work or at the pub or squash club, you tend to feel like the one who's excluded yourself.

A useful test is to ask yourself: How do I feel? Then apply the answer to your partner, and see if it fits with his behaviour. If he makes you feel neglected and shut out, perhaps it's because he feels that way himself. Then try talking about it. It may be that you could be more generous in your behaviour, or it may be that he needs to realize that the "exclusion" is happening only in his mind.

The last man described above guzzles alcohol for comfort, like a baby suckling at the breast; he has violent tantrums, is demanding and childish, and even calls his wife "mum". He is behaving with the jealous rage of a first child who sees his place usurped by the new baby. His behaviour is so extreme that it is doubtful whether his partner could help him to grow up and take responsibility for his adult self, even if she were aware of his jealousy. As it is, she is reacting – quite naturally – by getting angry with him and more protective of her baby, which will of course compound his feelings of rejection.

Here is another case of a man reverting to the behaviour of a jealous child:

"To be honest, it was like having three children – I could cope with the children, but I couldn't cope with him. His attitude to life and work seemed immature, and he had temper tantrums. He was in and out of jobs. I found I had to shoulder most of the responsibility for the home and children as well as work to pay the bills. I find a lot of men like their partners to work to contribute their share to the family income, but are not willing to do their fair share of the housework. Their day off work is a day off work, full stop. Then they wonder why we feel resentment."

And the following woman is still trying to come to terms with the fact that she has two "children":

"Right now is the most stable our relationship has ever been – but I look forward to returning to some form of work when our daughter goes to nursery school. I feel so empty and lonely at times. I'm feeling trapped most of the time, almost like being a prisoner in my own house. I never have any time to myself, never go out without my baby daughter. My life consists of cooking, cleaning, ironing, gardening and looking after my two babies – i.e. my partner and my daughter. I get so depressed and cry during the day. I keep telling myself that there must be more to life. I feel I have not lived enough. I'm adamant that I will return to open learning as soon as my daughter goes to nursery – and maybe regain some independence, rediscover my individuality. I feel this will be the best for everyone in the future."

Men rarely like to appear vulnerable. Generations of training have taught them that it's not masculine to show feelings that could be wounded. So when there is a problem in the relationship, a man will often refuse to acknowledge, let alone discuss it.

"I wanted more. I wanted someone who put me first, not the TA [Territorial Army]. I also wanted someone who would be there for the family. However, he was not willing to change. He would not talk about things that were going wrong in the relationship. Basically he stuck his head in the sand and hoped that the problems would go away, or that I would put up with things as they were. But I wasn't prepared to do that, and when I met my present husband he made me realize what I was missing, and that he could give me what I wanted."

Some women, like the one above, are lucky enough to find a second partner who has developed emotionally. Others, for the time being at least, become resentful and withdraw.

"I felt lonely and resentful."

"I became bitter, hostile, angry, resentful, depressed. He withdrew."

The numbers of single-parent families are steadily increasing: at the time of writing, one in five families nationally is looked after by just one parent. Nine out of ten single parents are women, and over half of these are living on less than £100 per week, which is 37 per cent of the income of a two-parent household. Increasing numbers of children are being brought up in long-term poverty. People become single parents for many reasons, but one of them is undoubtedly the fact that many men who become fathers, like those described here, are not equipped for parenthood. Divorce statistics show that the early years of parenthood are a particularly dangerous time for marriage.

What inadequacies of upbringing have allowed so many men to get out into the world without growing up? Little girls grow up watching their mothers, or childminders, or other paid help – usually female – care for the home and family, learning all the time how to do it themselves. Little boys have no such role model of what it is like to be a man, as the men are usually absent from the scene, out at work. If their fathers do not integrate with the family and take personal responsibility, how is the next generation of young men going to learn family skills? One woman points out that mothers often compound the problem. She says her husband had been thoroughly spoilt and cossetted by his mother, who "warmed his underpants on the radiator and squeezed his toothpaste on his brush!" Having been looked after all his life by his mum, who wouldn't allow him to lift a finger, this man expected the same treatment from his wife. Fortunately, she was able to make him understand that things had to change, and: "Our relationship became more equal, by which I mean my husband matured."

Some mothers do have a tendency to spoil their sons, perhaps because they are over-compensating for not being able to lavish affection on their own partners. If you recognize yourself doing this, just think carefully about the real meaning of that glibly used word "spoil", and remember that your son will probably one day be a parent himself. Are you helping him to grow up?

175

Putting the children first

Quite often, women respond to neglect by learning to do without the emotional support of their partners and becoming completely absorbed in motherhood.

"I became more wrapped up in motherhood. He became moody and more withdrawn than usual."

"Everything at the beginning felt great, but gradually disillusionment set in. I became very selfish towards my partner. He became very critical of my appearance and my apparent neglect of the housework, and didn't seem to understand how tired and bored I often felt. I rather lost interest in the world outside, as everything seemed to revolve around the children. I also lost interest in sex, although I usually went along with it to please my husband."

Sometimes this works – in a way. It becomes a marriage that's completely dominated by the children.

"I became more confident and less selfish. He didn't change. The children dominate our lives. Friends, parties, school, play school, toddlers' meetings, days out – most of our activities are for them, and we have to make a real effort to go out for us."

Children can be more loyal in their affections, and more appreciative than a partner:

"Because my husband loved me less and less, I seemed to love the children more. They loved me back unconditionally. Their love seems more rewarding somehow. They are more affectionate to me than my husband has been. They are more interested in me than he is."

"I realize that my husband is not affectionate enough for my liking, but I have all the affection I need from the children at the moment. I hope to improve things as they get older."

But they are also very demanding, and relating only to children leaves a lot of the adult self unsatisfied.

"I completely submerged my personality to look after my daughter."

"Deteriorated. Boredom, familiarity. We don't make enough time for us as a couple or as individuals. It's always the family. Romance – dead."

It's a downward spiral. Putting the children first means that communication between partners is neglected. A marriage that's held together just "for the sake of the children" rarely survives their growing up.

"I did see to the children's needs first before considering my husband. We stopped communicating our own needs and tended to blame each other for everything that went wrong."

"We grew to resent each other and grew further apart. Having had two children we were less of a family than we were before! He worked, I did everything else. We still had an active sex life and that was always very important to us both, but even that was not good really. In retrospect, mother love took over and I can see I loved my children far more than my husband, and we destroyed our marriage by not stemming the tide of creeping resentment and alienation."

"We have grown apart as the children have grown up. I feel totally redundant and not needed. Although my husband loves the children, his feelings towards me are indifferent."

This woman emerged from the years of devoting herself to single-handed childrearing to reassert her independence, which has upset the balance of things:

"For the first time in 14 years spent looking after five children, I've had time for myself, and I've expressed myself more. It has caused a lot of friction and seems to have fuelled his insecurities."

Is it a good idea to stay together "for the sake of the children"? Do they really benefit from being brought up in a loveless marriage? This woman's children hardly ever saw their father, who was always working or on the golf course. She was courageous enough to leave him, and now her children have a stepfather who loves to be with them:

"After having the children I would say we grew apart. He continued as before, whereas my life changed totally. I made friends who had children and my life basically revolved around them.

I think that because mine was an army family, and I went to boarding school for the majority of my childhood, I was desperate to have children of my own and not to make the mistakes my parents had made. It was me who wanted children and I plunged straight into three accidental pregnancies before realizing that there was a lot more to life than being with a man I didn't really love. I suddenly felt really trapped. He was working – with his independence well intact, he had a good social life without me and played golf in his leisure time. I seemed to be alone with the children doing all the family things.

My parents are still together after 27 years, yet they hate each other. My mother would say: you've made your bed, now lie in it. I was with my now ex-husband for seven years and I felt I put everything I had into the relationship before deciding to go it alone. That was two years ago. A year later I met an absolutely wonderful caring man who adores my three children, and who works to live, not lives to work, like my ex. We are very much in love and got married a month ago with a planned conception on the wedding night! We are totally involved with each other – he even has symptoms of pregnancy himself! We have a loving ready-made family, so most of the pitfalls have already been got through, and we are now very much both looking forward to a baby born of our love.

He has also been married before, and we both knew that this time we were ready for complete commitment. I feel very close to him and he to me and we have a wonderful life to look forward to together. This time it's definitely for keeps."

Three other women tell how they found empathy and a good father for their children in their second marriages:

"My first marriage ended in divorce. I was only 19 when I had my first child and having to take responsibility for this new life came as an extreme shock. I had post-natal depression – my husband didn't help at all – I was very possessive about my daughter and wouldn't let her out of my sight.

With my second husband it is the opposite, completely. We've grown together – almost sometimes as if we're one person. We've had our problems – he would never talk to me about his feelings – but he has learned to open up more, instead of bottling everything up. He is very loving, helpful, supportive and understanding (sounds too good to be true, doesn't it!). He loves my daughter and [has] treated her as his own from the off. I was very insecure in my first marriage, but I'm very content in my second!"

"I think we have settled down as a family more. Both my elder children from my first marriage have accepted my husband as their stepfather, and having our new baby has definitely been a bonus for us all."

"My present relationship with my second husband is totally different to that of my first marriage. My husband is a good father to my children. He puts me first and any problems we have he will always discuss. We always solve our problems as soon as possible rather than let them grow bigger."

And in the case of this single parent, separating has been a good thing for the whole family:

"We have been separated for three years – and now get on well! The children love their dad and he loves them, and I'm sure gives them more quality time and attention and support than he would have done had we been together. Our separation improved their relationship tremendously. The kids spend 2-3 days a week with him and the rest with me, and they are happy and well. He and I can finally connect again at the level where we began 10 years ago – as friends."

When all a man does for a family is finance it, a woman's only worry about leaving must be how to support herself and her children.

"We got to the stage where I felt he did nothing for us, except earn money, and there was no family life at all. I had had no support, no help, no sharing, and so I stopped cooking for him, because he was never there. We talked less. We couldn't even be bothered to make each other a cup of tea. I arranged social events, but he wasn't interested and didn't turn up. Our relationship deteriorated completely and his violent bad temper got worse. I told him he was destroying my love for him with his temper. I tried to involve him in our lives. I tried to talk to him. He didn't want to know."

Yet some choose to stay and lead separate lives.

"We live separate lives in the same house."

"We are now a working team. My husband pays the bills and I run the home and family. We lead quite separate lives and spend very little time together."

"The healing of our marriage"

Finally, one woman describes how she believes that for herself and her husband, parenthood will heal the wounds of the past:

"We both started facing up to our pasts. We were both abused as children. I was physically abused by my alcoholic father, and my mother, while knowing it was going on, did nothing to stop it, and even stopped me from talking about it. I was never even allowed to say that he took a drink.

My husband was illegitimate, and born on an island in the Highlands of Scotland. His mother married the first man who offered to take her away, to avoid the humiliation of being a single mother. My husband was raised as his grandparents' son and believed his mother to be his sister.

When his grandmother died, he was sent to live with his mother. He was six. He found out that she was his mother when he was ten. He suffered physical, mental, emotional and sexual abuse from his stepfather. His mother blamed him for all that happened, and kept saying she hated him.

Having a child of his own has enabled him to see himself as the victim, instead of the one who was to blame, and he is now seeking therapy. We both believe that this will be the start of the healing of our marriage."

Together with their child, this couple are making a courageous new start in life. Elsewhere in the survey, the same woman says that her greatest reservation about having a baby was that it would suffer just as she and her husband had done. This is not as illogical as it sounds, because abuse, like other behaviour, is often passed down from one generation to the next. This couple have broken the cycle.

 What are the best things about sharing parenthood?

For a lot of parents, sharing itself is the best thing. The single parent certainly has a huge burden of responsibility to bear, as does the mother whose partner is never there. Here are some answers that show the pleasure a common bond can bring:

"Because we are sharing parenthood, our children will hopefully grow into well balanced, loving and sharing adults themselves. We hope that our children succeed in whatever they do, but their happiness is most important and I think this will only be born of a happy upbringing."

"The way children make us want to hug and kiss them because they show unconditional love. Children make us realize how unselfish we can be."

"The antics of children. Laughter!"

"A common interest! I know it sounds boring, but we just love telling each other about the kids – little things they have said or done! A homely atmosphere and security."

"A more balanced input from both parents than we had in our childhoods. The child feels safe with either parent, having known them both."

"Joy at seeing the children grow, gain confidence, learn new skills. Having different priorities. Sometimes seeing things through the eyes of a child. All the extra physical touching."

"The best thing about sharing parenthood is having someone to share the bad times with. The time one of them ran away from home because he could not have his way over some trivial matter. The time one of them was arrested, at age 13, for shoplifting. The times they have had to be rushed to hospital for some emergency or other – and there have been several of those."

The saddest answers are the large number that come from those women who say they do not share parenthood, and not all of them are technically single parents. Many women feel that they are bringing up their families alone, because their partners fail to participate or show any interest. The only contribution they make is a financial one. One woman whose husband is in the Forces says wryly that Forces wives always bring up their children single-handed – it's part of the job.

Several women with partners who are good fathers mention how they would hate to look after their families single-handed.

"I just know I would not like to do it on my own and I admire anyone who has to. I love going out as a family, such as trips out to the beach or a picnic. Also, I love weekend mornings when we all have a cup of tea in our bed and talk about everything."

And a former single parent says:

"When you find someone to share the responsibility with, you feel like a whole person, not just a person who produced two children and is now expected to stop living until they have grown up and left home, and because I enjoy the responsibility now, my children are also more relaxed with me."

181

What are the worst things about parenthood?

For many women, the worst thing about parenthood is not sharing it:

"Not sharing it. I was a single parent to a five-year-old and a fifty-year-old."

"When it comes to the crunch, the mother has the nasty jobs to do."

The moral, emotional and financial responsibility of having children puts stress on many parents. They worry about their children's health and wellbeing, now and in the future, and about how to guide them through the difficult teenage years.

"Watching them make mistakes. Watching their innocence eroded by outside influences. Standing by while they suffer through their illnesses."

"Eldest daughter diagnosed with leukaemia at 3½, followed by brain haemorrhage at age 5. Tends to sort our your priorities and puts life into very clear perspective."

"Fear of the unknown, when maybe they have something wrong and you don't know what to do."

"Worrying about the children's schooling – we have moved house several times. Worrying about drugs, alcohol etc. and whether they will be sexually promiscuous. Worrying whether or not there will be work for them when they leave college etc."

"School reports; daughter getting pregnant at 18."

"The worry of what the world will be like when our children are ready to go out into the big world and set up their homes etc."

For some couples, the worst thing about being parents is their own lack of freedom and privacy.

"Not being able to have a conversation until the children have gone to bed, and not being able to be spontaneous when it comes to sex."

"Loss of individuality. Becoming someone's mum or dad and not a person. People assume that a mum has not got a brain or an opinion on world events, especially if she's at home all day."

"Lack of sleep. Hurried or missed meals. Not being able to talk to one another without being interrupted. No time for yourselves. Constant demands, physical and emotional. Constant stress and boredom."

A major cause of dissatisfaction with family life is the question of discipline. Lack of agreement and understanding on this subject causes bitter rows with and about the children.

"It's alright to chastise the children, but a different matter when your partner starts to lay down the law."

"The worst thing is when a child doesn't comply with your wishes, especially in a public place such as a restaurant or supermarket."

"Children trying to undermine our unity to meet their own ends!"

"We clashed in the past over punishments when the kids were younger. My husband was so strict, whereas I was easy-going. Trying to compromise."

"Fathers tend to put down boys – this causes the mother to fight back."

"Shouting at the children when they repeat doing something/not doing something you have told them about 200 times already. A lot of mums get cross with their children and spend a lot of time instructing and correcting them and little time enjoying having them about."

However, several couples say there are no drawbacks as long as parenthood is shared. One woman explains why this is so in her household:

"We have never argued about the way our children should be treated or brought up. In fact, there was an incident when our eldest son was being cheeky and both my husband and I slapped him at the same time! I feel sorry for our children because we have always presented a totally united front, and they have never been able to play us off one against the other."

It makes sense to work out a joint approach to discipline and to change or relax the rules only after you have agreed with your partner – in private – what the new rules should be.

INFIDELITY

Most contributors say *trust* is even more important in sustaining a marriage than love, but the marriage in which neither partner betrays that trust is becoming increasingly rare.

People have affairs when the spark of fantasy in their marriage dies. They need them to nourish their imaginative lives, to enable them to survive the mundane everyday. Forbidden intimacy and sexual excitement can bring extremes of passion and anguish because affairs are almost invariably doomed: star-crossed lovers hardly ever seem to take practical steps into domesticity.

If there is an affair in your marriage, how should you handle it? Should you face up to the painful truth that trust and magic are gone and try to rebuild your lives, or should you keep quiet, and hope that the lovely memory, or the gnawing jealousy, will eventually fade away?

About 50 per cent of contributors say they have either been unfaithful or have partners whom they know or strongly suspect have had affairs. Some who have been unfaithful themselves have kept their affairs secret from their partners. So it seems reasonable to assume that this survey bears out the result of previous surveys conducted by Relate and others, which suggest that there is adultery in between 60 and 75 per cent of the marriages investigated.

 Have you ever been unfaithful? If so, why did you have the affair?

Many answered "no", or "never"; a few expanded interestingly on their negative.

"No. I think there's a lot to be said for fidelity. I think it's sexy that two people can have a long-term relationship and continue to find each other desirable."

"I have had several men invite me to have affairs with them, but they have all been married. They were not able to offer me anything more than I already have, in fact a lot less, and I didn't fancy any of them. I have fancied other men and they have fancied me but I have never encouraged any of them into

185

having an affair because I value the relationship that I have with my husband and I would not want to hurt him. He doesn't deserve to be hurt."

"No, but I was very attracted not so long ago to another man who was divorced, but if it came to having an affair I would stay loyal to my husband."

"No, but I betrayed his trust by making a pass at someone else. It was pure lust. He refused (thank God), and I feel guilty even though nothing happened."

"I have never had a physical relationship with anyone other than my husband. I am deeply attracted to another man but honestly don't know, if the opportunity arose, whether I would be unfaithful."

Two other contributors, one male, one female, express a hint of curiosity:

"I have always been true. I look, but I don't touch. However, I would have an affair in the future if I got the chance."

"Never. Mind you, I've never had the offer."

A man of 75, obviously ill-at-ease with his sexuality, expresses himself with detachment and distaste:

"Three females offered me the use of their bodies but I could not rise to the occasion."

Contributors cited many reasons for having an affair; they fell broadly into two categories: those who wanted to experiment with other sexual partners, and a bigger group of people who were driven mainly by the desire for intimacy.

Intimacy

Most women and men in the survey who have had affairs were seeking intimacy – love, attraction, attention – that their marriages were failing to provide. They fell in love with their affair partners and many stayed in the marriage only for the sake of the children involved.

"Yes. I wanted to be loved and needed. I was in love with him, but I decided I could not risk losing custody of my daughter."

"Yes. I felt no passion with my husband and was in love with the other man. But I couldn't leave my husband because of the children."

"Yes, because I was needing attention and my life was in need of a general lift and a change. I believe I was in love but the affair ended because we both had young families."

"I had an affair because my marriage was at a low ebb. I was deeply in love, but I broke it off, as it would have broken up two homes."

"Four years ago I had a very serious affair that lasted some time. I was badly let down then and have never quite recovered. Though I do love my husband, I am not *in love* with him and have had to establish this so we can go on understanding each other. We both just about cope with it. He feels lack of affection, but I can't give it as I will always love someone else. I was going to leave him for this other man but would never have left my children."

This last case shows how very difficult it can be to decide what is really best for the children. Might they not be happier brought up by separated parents reconciled to their differences than as the "glue" sticking a loveless home together? Or was the affair based on fantasy, and has it provided the contributor with the "excuse" she needed for distancing herself from her husband?

For two women, their affairs gave them back a sense of their own individuality, which had been swamped under the roles of wife and mother.

"Yes, with a colleague I worked for for five years. We were in love. From the outset I said I would not leave my family. I encouraged him to find someone else because he was unhappy at home. He did. I was devastated. I realize how unrealistic romantic love is, but it is intoxicating. I felt my life was arranged around the family – the affair was my private time."

"Yes. It made me feel attractive and wanted and alive as a person instead of being just a wife and mother. I was in love. He chose to stay with his wife. I was heartbroken."

Next, two women tell why they are currently having affairs:

"Yes. I am having an affair because I need love and emotional security."

"Yes. Because I love him and have known him for 55 years. The affair started two years ago. My husband has no idea. He thinks, so he says, that no man would ever want me. I have actually had many offers. He knows so little about me that he thinks I'm not interested in men.

My lover is married and lives many miles away, so we don't see each other as often as we would like. He is also 'trapped' for financial reasons."

This last woman, living in a marriage destroyed after 19 years by her husband's alcoholism, started her affair aged 60. Her new-found intimacy with an old friend has clearly brought a lot of love and happiness into her life. She says that she would contemplate another affair in the future, but hopes she doesn't have to, because she wants this one to last. "It's not so easy to meet and fall in love." Hers is a story that could inspire many of the unhappy older contributors to this survey with new confidence.

And here is a moving contribution from a woman who thought she was happily married, until she fell in love with another woman. She describes her crisis of identity and the difficulty she and her husband have had in coming to terms with her new self.

"Somebody walked into my life and within six months my husband was no longer my best friend, the person I had needed for so long. Maybe we were married too young and at that age I saw my youth slipping away. But suddenly I was aware of myself as a person again (I never realized I had stopped considering myself as one). I was into clothes, fashion, music and doing things I hadn't bothered with for so long. I was totally out of control of my feelings even though it upset me and made me very sad. The relationship I developed with the other person was also so out of character for me that I had to cope with a new side to myself, previously unknown, unthought-of and very frightening.

Throughout my and my ex-husband's unhappiness we tried to do everything possible to keep the children in a steady situation. He continued to see them at least twice a week and always at weekends. After a lot of the bitterness had passed we continued to be together for birthdays and special events. Christmas has always been spent here, with my ex staying over for a night or two. A bizarre situation for many people to accept, but we have always felt that it was best for them. In many ways we have remained close. I know that in a disaster I can rely on him and vice-versa."

Sometimes it takes an affair to keep a poor marriage from breaking down altogether. In these next two stories, women use their fantasies of sexual intimacy to block out the mundane reality of their marriages.

"Yes. It started … when my husband went abroad to work and my children went to college. It lasted 10 years. I hungered for love and sex and a 'real' man. He was totally different from my husband. I felt I had to experience what a different man was like. My love for this man was all-consuming – the strongest thing I had ever felt in my life. It brought the greatest highs and the most indescribable pain. He was a male chauvinist, great fun, but, as I discovered, could not resist any woman, and I discovered he was sleeping with someone else while with me. He finished with me, because I was so distraught and clinging, and I was suicidal. A familiar story. I learned more from this than from any other experience, but I will never forget the 'highs', and would not have missed them."

Though she says she hungered for a "real" man, her affair has very strong overtones of fantasy. Her passion is as wild as her lover is unattainable: it is, as she says, "a familiar story". Destructive as it was, the affair has been absorbed and encompassed by the safe if boring reality of her marriage, to which she has returned, much enriched by having explored the full scope of her feelings. Without the safety net of her marriage, perhaps she might not have risked so much.

The woman above is nourished by the memory of her affair, but the next contributor feeds off hers in a very different way.

"Yes. I fell in real love for the first time in my adult life when I was 21. We still meet occasionally (I am now 42), but we made the decision not to destroy our families and have had no real physical relationship for many years now, in order to spare each other more hurt. Although now all our children have grown, we still feel we can't hurt our partners. I cry almost daily for my lover, but I treasure the fact that we were one for so long before we cooled it. No one will ever take the place he has in my heart. A love like ours only happens once in a lifetime. Who knows, when we're old and grey, we may still be together some day. Until then I will treasure my very precious private secret, and continue to use my very vivid imagination during lovemaking."

Hers is a morbid and sentimental fantasy, feeding off a need for tragedy. Surely it is one thing, waiting 21 years for your children to grow up and leave home, and quite another, waiting perhaps another 40 years in the hope that both "unwanted" partners might die off and leave you to reunite with your aged lover? This woman is weeping crocodile tears. If she wanted to, she could either improve her life with her husband, by making love to *him* instead of to a fantasy figure, or plan to start life afresh with her lover. However, she is probably most comfortable sheltering from the difficulties of reality in self-delusion.

These last two accounts make you wonder how much *all* extra-marital affairs are based on fantasy. If the state of being in love itself is an illusion (see page 5), then being in love with someone unattainable must be the height of illusion – and it certainly triggers the most poignant, acute emotions and the deepest swoons.

Sexual experiment

A smaller but significant number of contributors were sexually frustrated in their marriages and primarily out for some excitement:

"The need for good healthy sex prompted my affair. We weren't in love – both of us were committed elsewhere."

"Because my husband was a lousy lover. I thought I was in love each time, but it ended because it was only physical."

"I needed adventure. I thought I was in love with him and I still see him from time to time as a friend, and we both have deeper feelings for each other, which we manage to hide because we are both married with children and it would cause too much upset to pursue things. He is very tempting though!"

"I have had two affairs, with the same man, because he was an absolutely fantastic lover."

The next woman is the 77-year-old who has lived a life full of sexual frustration. Her husband has been impotent for 45 years. They are still together, despite complete incompatibility. If she had gone to live with her lover, maybe they could have helped each other and the relationship would not have ended so tragically.

"Yes, because during treatment for a nervous breakdown the psychiatrist recommended I should find a lover, because of my frustration – at the age of 45 I had never known what an orgasm was! I was 'in love' but did not love him. We were best friends for 20 years, but met only six times. We wrote long letters and phoned. He taught me that sex was FUN and LAUGHTER. He killed himself in the end. My husband condoned the affair and was not hurt – it lessened his guilt feelings over his failure."

In this last unusual case, sexual boredom led to a domestic triangle:

"Yes, I had an affair with another woman, but it became a threesome and my husband was in love with her too. We all lived together very happily for nearly 4 years until she decided she just wanted to love my husband.

We had the affair because my husband and I were going through a boring time sexually. A very dear friend of mine's marriage broke up and she had nowhere to live, so I offered her a room in our house. One evening she was upset and my husband put on some music and drew us all close together. We started to enjoy each other's bodies and love just grew from there. I was so in love with her and my husband, I felt complete.

It ended because she didn't love me any more. My husband and I went to Relate to save our marriage and I am glad to say that we did."

The answers to this question show that people have affairs when they meet someone who fulfils a lack in their prime relationships. The need may not even be consciously identified until the person comes along who can satisfy it, but it is surely there. This shows the importance of keeping intimacy alive in your relationship with good communication to affirm that you care. It also shows how we undervalue the importance of our imaginative lives. Taking your partner for granted in the role of husband, wife or parent and losing sight of the individual with emotional and sexual needs is leaving a gap that invites their fantasy to entertain someone else's appreciation and attention. In other words, each of the three people involved is responsible for the affair.

Q: Do you believe your partner is faithful?

This is a question about openness and self-delusion. In any marriage you have to decide between honesty, which may sometimes bring pain and difficulty, and the policy of turning a blind eye for the sake of a superficial truce.

Some give strong reasons for believing their partners are faithful.

"Yes, totally. We've talked about faithfulness etc. and we both truly believe that it would be the end of our relationship if either was unfaithful."

"Yes. It was something we agreed we were pleased about and discussed when my husband knew he was dying."

"Yes. He sowed enough wild oats before we met for him to be sure he wanted to marry me. I have never doubted his fidelity despite his having worked away from home on numerous occasions during our marriage."

"Yes, he was faithful. He was glued inside his slippers, which were glued to the carpet in front of his shrine – the telly."

Others are less sure:

"Yes. But I'm not naive and I realize that life changes all the time, and you have to work hard at it if you want to make it work successfully. I think my husband is desirable and there are plenty of others who think so too!"

"Yes I do! Unfortunately, most women do!"

Others know their partners have been unfaithful, and are finding out how to deal with it as a couple (page 198), but many who have no proof are left in the limbo-land of varying degrees of suspicion.

"We don't often bring out the best in each other any more. My husband works away for 45 days, and is then home on leave for about 20 days, which is very difficult to adjust to. Our emotions are therefore probably intensified during the time that he is at home. He says he needs to go out and have some freedom while he's on leave, which I try to understand, but he doesn't seem to appreciate that I would like him to stay at home with me a bit more. He also drinks rather heavily, which creates tension between us, and we do argue quite a lot. I have a problem in trusting him too. I have no absolute or concrete evidence that there is or has been someone else, but numerous incidents have made me very suspicious. I know I'll never get to the bottom of it because he denies that he's done anything wrong, but I feel deep down that my suspicions are not without substance."

"I believe he has been unfaithful, probably a few times, but not serious affairs. He will not own up."

"I believe he is faithful even though he has this friend I know would like to go to bed with him. I don't think he could – I would have to be out of his life first."

"I believe he is faithful but I know he could be tempted. He had affairs before, when he was going out with his previous girlfriend – while he was at sea, with other men's wives."

"Yes, I do now. I used to be very suspicious but he's proved it to me and I do believe him now."

"I don't know whether my husband has slept with this friend of ours. She sent signals to him over several years."

In a relationship that's based on trust, suspicion is the worst kind of cancer. There is a strong sense of self-delusion in many of the answers above, and this is probably the only thing that's holding these marriages together.

 If he or she has had an affair, how did you find out?

This section is about the desirability, or otherwise, of confronting the truth. If your partner is leaving clues, do you pursue them or ignore them? If you have had an affair, do you tell?

Some found out from other people:

"I suspected because of his neglectful, hurtful behaviour. I had an anonymous obscene phonecall from a 'friend', telling me about the affair."

"He had a lover for two years. I was unaware of this until I got a letter anonymously and found some cards and condoms."

These answers pose a very difficult question: what is a friend to do who knows? An anonymous message revealing the truth will undoubtedly cause more hurt than a frank talk − but is it any business of the "friend's"? Self deception is often an important part of the equation in marriage, and an outsider who interferes is likely to meet with anger and rejection.

The woman on page 97 whose husband has been leading a double life in the Far East while she stays at home with her grown-up daughters blames friends for not putting her in the picture. In fact she has only her own lack of concern for her husband to blame − that and a very poor imagination.

Most contributors who were cheated on were told by their partners, either directly in words, or indirectly, through odd behaviour.

"Usually because he was so bad at covering up after himself and the people used to ring up at home."

"I was suspicious because he kept mentioning a particular woman's name. I pointed this out and asked him if he was having an affair, but he denied it. He doesn't know I've had an affair and I shall never tell him! I wish sex with him could be as good as it was with my lover."

"He wasn't making love. I was suspicious. I said: 'Are you getting depressed? It's either that, or there's someone else.' Then he told me."

"She made excuses as to why she had stayed out – they weren't very believable. She seemed to change and behave out of character."

"I know because he washes more often, gets a glazed look in his eye."

"I suspected he was being unfaithful – late home, hazy excuses etc., little notes – funny smells."

People leave clues because the urge to confess is often a strong temptation, seriously rivalling the need for secrecy. Being in love gives a feeling of increased self-worth that is very difficult not to flaunt. The secret can become a burden in many ways, and if the unfaithful partner is afraid of confrontation, letting it slip out in "clues" is a way of handing over the responsibility for discovery to the other person. It's like saying: "Here's the evidence – this is what I'm doing – now it's up to you whether you want to make an issue out of it or not." Providing your partner with evidence of your unfaithfulness is a small gesture towards absolving your own guilty conscience. Many partners who are cheated choose to ignore the evidence, thus tacitly condoning the affair. Some marriages are held together precisely because one partner is prepared to turn a blind eye.

In the next story, the husband's guilty conscience wouldn't allow him to have his cake and eat it – quite literally! – and it was this that gave his wife the clue.

"In February 1988 my 18-year-old son died in a car crash. I had had him before I met my husband, and he had been brought up by my parents; his name was J. My husband had been extremely close to him, and I put his mood changes down to J's death. It wasn't until April that I really thought something was wrong. He was having severe mood changes, but the one thing that made me suspicious was that he stopped eating my cakes. Whenever he got back from a trip, he always wanted me to have homemade cake for him. That was the first inkling I had. I asked him a couple of times, but he denied having an affair.

In June that year I went with him on a seven-day trip to the Far East. Things started to improve – he seemed to be 'with me' again emotionally. We were staying in Hong Kong and had a wonderful day shopping and had been out for a meal in the evening. When we went to bed I had (I don't really know how to describe it) a sort of dream, but I felt awake – it was maybe unconscious thoughts coming to the surface. I knew if I looked inside his briefcase, and in his log book (something I had never done before), I would find something. In the morning, while we were having breakfast, I made an excuse to go back to the room. I looked in his briefcase, and in his log book was a girl's address. I felt so sick. When he came to the room I confronted him. He admitted it, but said she was 'just a friend'. He was glad I had found out, it was a relief, and he said he was going to stop seeing her. But he didn't. It was on and off for 15 months. He didn't want to live with her, but couldn't stop seeing her. I decided to end it when she became pregnant. He no longer sees her. I think, what a tragedy – all the people who were hurt, especially the children. It was their pain I could hardly bear."

In many cases, the flood of relief and guilt at being found out would have ended the affair, but in this instance, the husband felt free to continue seeing his lover because their relationship was now "above board" and, for 15 months at least, tolerated by his wife.

Those 15 painful months were probably the undoing of this marriage. When she could suffer the affair no longer, her husband left his lover, even though he was now bound to her by their unborn child. But by that time it was too late to save the marriage, because the period of uncertainty had worn away at their feelings for one another.

The next woman is currently suffering an anguish of uncertainty and suspicion. Fear of discovering her husband is having an affair is keeping her paralysed, as they drift further and further apart.

"We were very much in love when we got married [29 years ago]. Our sex life has been great over the years. It now seems over a period of four years that we are like strangers. Our love has died. We don't have sex any more. I cry to myself! I tried to reach out. Maybe he has someone else. It looks like we will part. Maybe divorce?"

It could well be that this man has transferred his love elsewhere. But his wife has not got to the bottom of it. She seems to be suffering in silence, in an attempt to sit it out. If he is having an affair, this is a dangerous gamble, relying on the other woman ending the relationship. The husband is in a very strong position. With a wife who will ask no questions, come what may, he is free to behave exactly as he wishes. Why should he end either his affair or his marriage, as long as he is able to keep both? In the meantime, his wife's confidence and self-respect are draining away.

If she opens up to him, she will bring the affair into crisis and give their marriage a fresh chance. She needs to restore proper communication, or, even if the affair does end, there will be too much unspoken hurt between them to allow the real closeness she craves.

Confrontation in this situation is a positive way of saying you care about the health of your marriage. Confrontation need not mean an almighty and destructive stream of resentment and accusation (see page 199). The more realistically you view the situation and express your concern that you have drifted apart, your love, your fear and the loneliness of living with the torture of suspicion, the more likely your partner is to listen and to open up himself. Affairs do not happen unless something is lacking in a relationship (see page 186), and to try to discover together what this is means that you are taking responsibility for your share of what has gone wrong.

Facing up to a painful truth takes courage. But exercising courage does in itself give strength, and courage and strength fuel each other. If your relationship is drifting and is in need of a complete overhaul, you will feel stronger as soon as you get a grip on the situation and start taking control of your own part in it. If your partner feels guilt and remorse for being unfaithful to you, this will work in your favour if you want to rebuild your relationship. You will have to work through your needs realistically, which will clear the way and give you the chance to grow close again.

 How did the affair (yours or his/hers) change your relationship?

An affair may be necessary to fulfil the needs of an individual that are not satisfied by the marriage partner, but it very often diminishes the marriage still further.

"Trust went – things were never quite the same."

"It has devastated me. I can't eat properly, concentrate properly, or do anything. I feel cheated by my husband and by the woman who was my best friend, and very hurt."

"Knowing that my partner has a female friend who wants to go to bed with him has taken away a little of the love I felt – it's made me fight harder – it's also made me a little indifferent – but I think that this is self-protection."

"He never trusted me again and I think he stopped loving me. I thought if he really cared about me he would have tried to make me love him again. He didn't, and I eventually stopped loving him."

"It is making me realize my husband is the wrong man for me."

"I no longer want sex with my husband."

"I needed to have affairs because my husband was such a lousy lover. They made me realize I didn't love him."

"After we had both had affairs, life became more mundane, the sparkle gone. Sex life non-existent."

"Mine changed things dramatically. Things just don't seem as stable. I was his virgin bride. I fell from the pedestal. Things are still shaky."

"He had several short relationships in our time together and it just wore me down slowly over the years. I lost all respect for myself."

"His affair has damaged our relationship beyond belief. It has killed my feelings for him."

"My affair made me very much more unhappy at home."

"I had terrible guilt feelings, which eventually made me value my marriage a lot more – though my mind still drifts back."

"It has left me feeling very insecure at times, and wondering why, after nearly two years, it still hurts and continues to cause me a few problems."

Many plod on in the wake of an affair, leading a kind of half-life, clinging to the empty husk of their marriage and just waiting numbly for the hurt to go away. The next woman has taken the courageous decision to work through her pain to try and bring back life and love into her marriage.

"It has totally changed our relationship. I am devastated, depressed, lonely, untrusting, suspicious, jealous to the point of insanity, but I am trying to overcome everything and love him more than before. I don't want to lose him.

I am going through an extremely delicate stage of my marriage, trying to rebuild everything I thought I already had, but discovered I didn't have. Finding out about my husband's affair, and his general infidelity, has been earth-shattering, and I will never fully recover. I am being counselled, but it will take years to get these thoughts out of my mind.

The worst aspect of it is realizing that the man I have known for 34 years and lived with for 25 years has deceived me beyond my wildest dreams. Sometimes I cannot really believe that he did, but I know it's true. The humiliation of finding out, and thinking back to the times when we were together and he was sleeping with another woman, is just indescribable. I feel a dreadful loathing of all the people I thought were my friends, and who knew what was going on, but didn't tell me. I can never forgive them that. I am trying hard to forgive my husband and I am trying to remain the loving wife, but it is the hardest thing I've ever had to do."

Other contributors have taken the same positive action, working out between them or with the help of a counsellor what went wrong, resolving their problems, and gradually rebuilding each other's trust. The process may take years, and the wounds may never heal completely, but if both parties have the desire and energy to re-commit themselves, they can work towards a much richer life and a deeper understanding. The following couples are attempting to get closer again:

"I suppose I had some understanding of our circumstances when our relationship seemed to be breaking down – after all, I'd had an affair myself, so I couldn't criticize! When we got back together again it was on the understanding that we would work at our marriage, not play at it."

"The affair was a threesome with my best friend. It left my husband feeling that I only half loved him, because I was so much in love with her, and it left me feeling the same about him. Also, he felt he could never satisfy me the way another woman can. We had to rebuild trust between us."

"It made me feel insecure and deeply hurt. Still affects me. It brought us closer as we bothered to resolve the problems that caused the affair. It happened during the first years of our marriage and now we are celebrating our 31st anniversary."

"I was very upset but determined to win her back and after 5–6 years of turbulence, when what kept us together was our own very good sex life, she was able to say she loved me."

"Her affair made me jealous, but eventually brought us closer."

"When my husband had his affair, he actually left me for three weeks. As he was working away from home at the time, very few people really knew the situation. I don't know how I coped, but I did. I had forgotten how much I loved him. But instead of going mad, I just told him that he had time to sort things out before making a decision. It worked – he came back, and since then we have had a wonderful relationship. We set about putting things right and rekindled the old feelings. The biggest thing was to start talking again. It hasn't always been easy, but we're both glad we had a second chance."

This last woman's calm, her inner strength and her realistic approach at a time of severe crisis were what gave her marriage a second chance. She stood her ground, kept her dignity, and allowed her husband to keep his by giving him the time and freedom to make his own choice. This immensely positive and creative attitude has proved a fruitful foundation for a new phase of married life; it would also have given her the courage to face life alone had her husband not been won back by his admiration and respect.

For a significant minority who were sexually frustrated in their marriages, their affairs gave a satisfaction that spilled into life at home, making the marriage more pleasant and easier to live with.

"My affair enhanced my relationship. It made me better to live with as I was having my sexual needs met elsewhere."

"I became more tolerant of our sexless marriage and was able to cope better without my former depression, having discovered what had been missing."

"It improved our sex life."

One woman's affair made her value her husband more:

"My affair made me feel good, but then generally [made me] reflect on my marriage and my relationship with my husband. I realized I didn't want to lose him – the risk was too great. I value life much more now; the affair made me take stock of the situation."

Pretty well the only conclusion that can be drawn about the effects of infidelity on marriage is that they are wildly unpredictable and likely to be devastating. So, if the failings in your marriage coincide with meeting someone who fills in the blanks in your life and you sustain yourself temporarily with an affair, should you keep it to yourself or tell your partner once it is all over?

The answer must depend on how you want your marriage to work. If you are content to have it ticking along in the background of your life, you will find it more comfortable to keep your memories to yourself, in the knowledge that changing nothing in the marriage will probably mean other affairs in the future. If the ending of your affair has brought relief and remorse, you may also decide to keep quiet to spare your partner – in fact the realization of how close you came to losing each other could make you more appreciative of and protective towards the other person. But if your affair has enabled you to identify flaws in your marriage that you want to try to make good, then openness is the only policy that will give both your integrity and your marriage a fresh chance.

If you choose openness, be prepared to take full responsibility for your actions and for your partner's hurt. Sometimes people are driven to tell all purely out of a desire to confess and be rid of the burden of a guilty secret. Because they know they will feel better having got it off their chests, they imagine their partners will understand immediately that it is no longer an issue and absolve them of guilt. This is unlikely to be the case! If you are unsure of what your partner's reaction might be, try to imagine how you would feel if the roles were reversed.

FIRST-HAND ADVICE

Many of the contributors to this book didn't only fill in the questionnaire, they wrote long and fascinating letters about their lives – one woman wrote 20 pages! The extracts in this chapter have been chosen for their usefulness, as insights into married life hard-won by trial and error. The sometimes conflicting points of view show how important it is not just to think ahead and be aware of all the options, but to choose an individual path that suits the unique qualities of your own relationship.

 What one piece of advice would you pass on to other people that you have learned from your experience?

This question elicited a lot of good sense, although in many instances a lot more than only one piece of advice was given! Contributors' advice fell smoothly into five categories. They wrote about factors to consider before deciding to have a family; about planning conception and looking after babies; about bringing up children; about togetherness and communication; and about putting one's partner first.

Factors to consider before deciding to have a family

"Make sure it's what you both want. Make sure your partner is strong enough emotionally to be completely leaned on while the wife is physically and emotionally vulnerable. Does the husband like and want children? If not, then don't think everything will be alright when the baby is born – it won't."

"I think partners should have a long talk about why they want children, how many they both want, and how they expect their lives to change as a result. Things like sharing housework and childcare, going back to work full- or part-time, should also be discussed in advance, so that neither partner is in any doubt about how the other one feels or what they expect. This also provides a basis for negotiation in the future."

"That a child, children, mean a change – a change in yourself, your partner, your relationship, in your way of life. It should be a joyous experience, but if you haven't realistically thought about it, talked about it, that change can be devastating – be aware."

"Be sure you understand the changes a baby will make to your life, and that your love is deep enough to stand the pressure. It is not easy adjusting. The most important thing is never to forget your partner is a person in his/her own right and not just an extension of the baby. Make time for each other and TALK!"

"Think carefully about how having children can change your relationship and be prepared to work hard at it. I think the baby stage causes the most problems between a couple, so be determined to make things work, in the knowledge that it gets easier to go out and do things together as a family as the children get older."

"You've *both* got to want them, *really* want them, because they need your *total* love and commitment day and night. The responsibility is heavy – you need a lot of energy and, at times when you're at your lowest ebb and most tired, the fact that you did really want them is all you've got to fall back on. A safety valve is the knowledge that someone else loves them as much as you do and can take over the responsibility for a while."

"Have children because you want to have them, not because you feel you ought and are under pressure from your family."

"Do everything, but *everything* else first. Once you have a family, you have to be very selfless – therefore, have your selfish time first. Travel, party, do whatever it is, and get it out of your system, and only then settle down, because once you start a family you are (or should be) tied for good."

"Don't even consider a family unless you have agreed how they are going to be brought up – including what rules you will make when they are teenagers. (Hard to imagine when you're 20!)"

"Really discuss if you want children and are ready to have them. We went wrong as he was working at night, and never saw the children. If you are a career woman you have to work twice as hard to make things right between you and your partner. He wanted his independence and no responsibilities."

"The most important thing is support. Both parents must want a baby. I would rather not have had the children than put them through all the rows and hate that develops when the relationship breaks down. Separation and divorce only hurt the people you are supposed to be helping to grow up: the children."

"Most important that a couple get to know one another thoroughly before children are contemplated, because most men I think have a 'little boy lost' attitude to married life and always need to be mothered, and when they see their children getting all the fuss they do tend to get jealous.

My husband can cope with little children, but he finds it difficult to relate to teenagers and cannot cope with the fact that his family are growing up.

I do think a couple have to agree from the onset on discipline, or upbringing of children will be difficult. I was lucky in this respect. I had control during the day and he always backed me up."

"G.K. Chesterton said: 'Never have a child until you can cease to be one yourself.' Never was a truer word spoken! (I was a single parent to a five-year-old and a fifty-year-old.)"

"Make sure your partner really wants a family. As a woman, remember that ultimately the responsibility of work and of children falls on you."

"Be absolutely sure that you both want a family. Children are a big commitment and looking after them is the responsibility of both parents. I also feel that women should not feel guilty about going back to work after having children. I personally feel that I am a better mother to my children than I would have been if I was at home with them all the time. My children are both very happy – bright and loving, and have no problems associating themselves with both adults and other children."

"Be honest with each other. Share chores equally. Listen to what your partner has to say. Have a laugh at yourself. Build up your own esteem by doing your own things. Have a good talk over the roles each of you will play when the baby arrives."

"Never have a baby as a means of bringing you closer. If there are problems, these will more than likely increase. Don't use a baby as an excuse for getting married – it must cause resentment."

"Become parents because you *both want to*, not because one of you feels it's going to bring you closer together or solve any problems you are having as a couple."

"Children can only bring you closer together if your relationship is good in the first place. It's important to retain your own identity and not be just mother and wife."

203

"Don't have children to bring your relationship together, because it does distance you for a while. You have to be totally committed, as being a parent is very hard work and whatever you do you will always feel you should have done more."

"Having children can bring you closer and force you further apart. Working together in bringing them up and sharing hopes and disappointments brings closeness. Disagreeing over the children can cause major rifts, and is frequently unavoidable."

"Listen and believe your friends when they tell you what it's like. Your child *will* be the same. In fact we borrowed friends' children straight from work on a Friday night and it gave us a good insight. Spend time playing with children as it doesn't always come naturally."

"Go for it when you think you want a family. I hear a lot of couples talking about their mortgage commitment, about giving up their career, about wanting this or that . . . well, they're not ready to start a family. They are far too materialistic. Yes, it is expensive bringing up a family, but the pleasure is immeasurable."

"Prepare yourself for the worst – if you can't have children, will you still love each other? Some people want children more than a partner – talk about it!

Be prepared to work hard and plan a sleeping/feeding routine for your baby if you want time to yourselves. If you pick the baby up every time it cries, and it cries when you're just off out on a special evening – you won't go – you have made your own problem. So talk about how you will actually look after the baby from day to day.

Having a family is not like going for a new job ... if you leave half way through, someone will be hurt, so talk, talk, talk, and read until you can't read any more – do your best to make sure it's what you want, then make sure it's fun!

I think the saddest thing is that there is a need for this kind of book. Society is falling apart. All the pressures on modern man and woman mean that they need help. The trouble is that lots of our friends, *young* people, need help now – God knows if they will manage another 20 or so years. I think it's because nobody takes anything seriously any more – everything – marriage, the family – it all comes with an opt-out clause. Our motto is 'work hard and play hard'. Lots of our friends want bigger and better things all the time – promotion, bigger houses, more money. We have ordinary jobs and no great ambitions. We just strive for 'happier' – being alive seems reward enough. I think of Molière: 'Il faut cultiver notre jardin.'"

On planning a family and looking after a baby

"Don't make other major changes at the same time. We made the mistake of buying a new house and moving when I was seven months pregnant. All that stress! We also made a big mistake in choosing the new house. Being used to working, passing shops etc., we didn't realize how important it would be to me, at home all day, to have shops, doctor, playground nearby. I was very isolated. How much better it would have been to stay where we were settled. We would have got used to the loss of earnings more easily, and had friends nearby for support.

All our babies were planned, but I made sure we never had another winter baby again. It takes ages to organize a baby for outings when he needs wrapping up warmly. Night feeds are bleak and the day seems more depressing if your partner is working late and it gets darker earlier. Christmas is very expensive – doubly so if a child's birthday falls near it, and there is boredom for the child who has outgrown all his toys by summertime. My second baby was born in June. It was so much easier and more pleasurable to take him out and about, even with a toddler in tow.

Dad must be involved with nappies etc. from the start, otherwise you will easily fall into a pattern with resentments building up – but his needs must be appreciated too. When my husband walked through the door after work, he was obviously tired, hungry, might have had a bad day, and wanted to flop for a while. I used to think: great! Reinforcements! And if I had had a bad day, I expected him to take over the reins. It has taken us years to get it right. I now don't expect much of him when he's worked late, but at weekends, we share the responsibilities. I am lucky that my husband enjoys cooking, so while I bathe a child or read a story, he will be preparing a meal. Being a parent is hell – but we love it!"

"Never marry anyone with a plan to change them. My husband has always helped with the babies and the housework. I am very, very lucky. Lots of women I know grow to resent or hate partners who think that childcare is the sole responsibility of their wives and refuse to change their lifestyle at all, but expect their wives to sacrifice everything.

I wish I'd had more idea of what to expect, as I had no experience of babies before I had my own.

Talk to each other – don't bottle your feelings up. Read lots of baby books and pregnancy books, and include your partner as much as possible.

Don't regard the baby as 'china' that will break if anyone else holds him. Let anyone (within reason) feed, hold and change the baby – and don't forget partners need cuddles as well. Don't worry about the housework, as long as clothes are clean and meals are good and regular. Don't attempt to be superwoman – take each day as it comes and get to know your baby – most of all, enjoy it."

"Let dad spend time looking after the baby on his own and getting to know him/her. Sharing as a threesome is the best-ever experience!"

"Looking after a baby should come naturally, so don't worry about what the textbooks say, just go with what you feel is right for your baby. No one knows your baby quite like you do, so don't be fobbed off by GPs etc."

"During the first couple of years try to keep telling yourself that the baby will eventually sleep one day – tiredness is an awful thing, it can make you feel so low."

On bringing up children

This first contribution comes from a wise woman of 79 who has been married four times. She apologises for the state of her long, entertaining and very thought-provoking letter: the pages are stained with tea and currant cake, as she is writing sitting up in bed, recovering from an illness. She also apologises for not having returned her questionnaire sooner: she has been going through a crisis because her husband is having an affair with the social worker he is consulting about his marriage problems. Here are some of the points that she makes:

"Take care of your children but don't own them. They are yours for life if you make friends with them and do not dominate them.

I do believe the parents' marriage has a great effect upon the children's marriages, because in a happy marriage, problems concerning any member of the family can be brought into the open and discussed. I certainly believe psychology should be taught in schools. I think a better understanding of others and of oneself would be a benefit in marriage.

The biggest success in my life has been with my daughters. We are so close that I could always talk to them about difficulties in my marriages, and they turn to me as well. I don't think it a good idea for parents to call each other mum and dad, because I think children should be brought up realizing that parents are people with their own feelings and thoughts – interesting people with other thoughts besides caring for offspring. Then lifelong friendships can develop between you.

As a girl, I grumbled to my father that I was bored. His reply I remember still: 'Well, my girl, if you are bored, think what you do to other people!' I've never been bored since!

I think that truthfulness and honesty is essential in married life. If trust goes, then happiness goes too. I always told my children that however bad the truth was, we could get over it together and win, but lying lost trust and belief for ever.

I've looked and listened and learned in life, and so many young people come to me for help, and I feel honoured that they do."

The next contribution comes from a devout Catholic who has eight living children.

"Children are blessings, not something you cannot afford. They are in fact the future doctors, lawyers etc., who will enhance the society in which we live.

We found our happiness in our children, and would never have found our own happiness without them. Love is what binds us together as a family, and despite all the many trials and tribulations we have had, we have been drawn together in deeper unity. The year when our daughter, T, was critically ill, when my husband was unemployed after working for the same firm for 18 years, and when I was expecting our ninth child was, according to human standards, an impossible situation. God sustained us through these difficult years, especially when T died aged 18. We were, during those years of suffering, enriched. We have always been blessed in our friends. Our lives are interesting and exciting and now we enjoy our nine grandchildren. Whatever has happened in our children's lives, we have always been there to stand by them and they have known that they could come to us in their need.

Being ourselves, being with one another, having a sense of humour, not letting things rankle, getting on with life and with whatever life presents to us, sums up the vocation of marriage. LOVE CONQUERS ALL!"

"The task of bringing up children does not ease as they get older – the teen years can prove very difficult for parents and children alike. We have experienced some traumatic situations with both our daughters, but thankfully, because of our support for one another, have [managed to] sort things out without too many lasting effects. We still offer our daughters direction and I think this is very important because it shows them that we still care, even though they are young adults themselves.

From the word go, I believe that children must be taught the basics of right and wrong, given your time and shown lots of love.

I have a very rewarding relationship with both my daughters. We discuss anything and everything. They trust and confide in me and tell me I'm their best friend."

"Try to compromise. Support each other. Try to have at least one meal a day at table. Show affection. Get a babysitter and go out. Don't store up problems."

"Be prepared to adapt. Look beyond any immediate problems and remember that you are still the same two people who fell in love and that a time will come in the future when the problem is over, i.e. the problem is temporary and the couple is permanent, not the other way round.

Do what works for you, especially when it comes to sleepless nights. Share beds, change beds, take shifts – you need to sleep or your problems mount. When you're niggly through lack of sleep you blame each other; when you're refreshed you can be more positive.

Set time aside for yourselves – take offers of babysitters. If the baby is sleeping – forget the housework and rediscover your passion! Remember, you are individuals, not just parents."

"I believe it is important for couples to have a regular break from the children and get out on their own one evening a week, or go away for the weekend if babysitting is available. This helps them to keep in touch with one another and remember why they fell in love in the first place. One of our problems was that we hardly ever went out when the children were small, and in the end it became a real effort for me to go anywhere at night! I used to feel as if everybody but me was having fun, which caused further resentment of my husband, who had a reasonable social life at work."

"Not to worry if your child doesn't do things when and how the books say. All children are different. Also, however bad it seems at first, it does get better! Some of the marriages I have seen break up are as a direct result of the pressures parenthood brings. Although I don't like to generalize, usually it's because the husband sees the children as his wife's sole responsibility, even down to never changing nappies or getting up in the night. The excuse that they work all day is not valid, as I work harder now I am at home with two children than I ever have before. I have been really surprised by how many men think they are doing their partner a 'favour' by playing with or taking out their own children. My own husband thinks nothing of taking one or both children away camping for a night or two to friends in order to give me some valuable time on my own. His attitude is a vital ingredient in the success of our marriage."

"We lack the skills of raising families that we would have learned naturally in a supported extended family environment. One can recreate this atmosphere to an extent with friends, but it does not have the same depth.

I found it hard to answer the questions on my husband's thoughts and feelings on parenthood, as like most men he is not emotionally revealing in the way that women are. Men work it all out to avoid expressing what they feel in words. There are a lot of unsaid things in the impact of parenthood on men. But in our marriage, being involved together in childbirth and childrearing has broken down some of the barriers between being a man and being a woman."

"I think I resent the amount of freedom that my husband has in not being tied to the children like I am. For example, he goes out whenever he likes when he's not working; however, if I want to go out, it takes so much planning and organization that it detracts from any enjoyment at getting out. We rarely go out together these days – I think it would do us good if we did."

"At the risk of upsetting feminists I cannot understand why women have children and go straight back to work. Children need two parents and it certainly is a good thing for one of them to be at home, particularly in the pre-school years. We need to persuade employers that fathers might like to spend some time caring for children and we need more after-school activities to avoid so many latch-key children. Although my children are now in their teens, I still feel I have to be at home when they get in from school, more to act as a referee than for any other reason."

"The angelic bundle you can't believe will ever be anything other than perfection will at times drive you to insanity – and when and if you finally say or do something you shouldn't, it's not the end of the world. Also, if they fall from grace, or never become achievers – you love them just the same!"

"The Open University courses like The Pre-school Child, and Children Five to Ten Years, are excellent because they provide insight into the child's point of view and help you to avoid conflict with the children. Join mother and toddler groups to prevent the isolation that some mothers feel: over the years you can make wonderful friendships with families. It's good to have friends like these you can rely on to leave your children with in emergencies."

This next contribution comes from a man who is divorced, but remains on good terms with his ex-wife and sees his children regularly:

"It seems to me that no matter what difficulties one goes through along the way, in the long run any regrets about having children disappear and are replaced by happy memories and a feeling of having something 'eternal' to show for our relatively few years in this life."

Here are some comments on discipline and arguing:

"Stick together on discipline, table manners etc. and don't let the children play you off one against the other."

"Most things are not worth arguing over. But if you feel strongly enough, say your piece, then leave it. Don't keep picking at your partner over the next hours, days, weeks. Don't argue about behaviour in front of the children. They quickly learn to use it!"

"You have to be firm and sometimes soft. Lots of love and cuddles and listen to what they have to say. A quick slap is more effective *immediately*, than a threat. Try not to row in their hearing."

"Always agree to back each other up in front of the children."

On togetherness and communication

"Keeping love alive is like keeping a fire going – it needs the correct fuel, regular attendance, and the dead ash cleaning out. In other words, don't kindle up dead stuff, try to forgive and forget."

"Talk about your feelings and problems before they escalate out of hand."

"We come from very similar backgrounds – both sets of parents were happily married. Over the years we've learned that communication and compromise have been two key factors in a happy marriage and family life. We show our love for each other (all four of us) and give each other a lot of time. Listening and giving people your time and interest is so important, no matter what their age. Our children are very proud of us and love us dearly – what more could parents wish for?"

"Tolerance. No marriage is perfect and you aren't always going to agree, or even like some of the things your partner does. If you get worked up and row over things before you start a family, it'll be much worse after you've got children. Tolerance doesn't mean you always have to give in to keep the peace, but talk things through – it's much worse keeping quiet and having things eating away inside you.

I think it's important to be open with one another. It's not always easy, especially when you're first married. I can remember lying in bed, thinking: I don't like what he's doing, and having to really pluck up courage to say so. We talk a lot in bed (not about what I like and don't like, as he knows me well enough now). It's a chance to cuddle and go over the day's happenings or problems without the interruptions of children or television. I value this time together, even when I'm very tired."

"Me and my husband are good friends, we're close, we rely on each other and support each other, we communicate well. But we don't expect too much from each other. I feel the most important thing we give each other is space to be ourselves."

"It's much better to try and be easy-going and enjoy each other's company without expecting to be ecstatically happy and constantly in love as you were at the beginning. If you do have quarrels, always try and calm down and talk it out later, and listen to each other. Communication is crucial to understanding each other."

"I tell my children: share yourself – don't keep yourself to yourself. Talk to your partners. Find out what pleases them and makes them happy. Love must be poured out in order to get it back. Every member of the family pours love into the family unit so that you and they are surrounded by love. If one person puts in just a little, there is less for the others."

"Keep short accounts with each other. We never sleep without talking through and sorting out problems and usually pray together each night.
One of the reasons our marriage works is the total trust we have in each other – so we have always felt able to share our time with other people. Too

many couples become obsessed with one another, so that their relationship becomes unbalanced and possessive, producing problems."

"Listen to each other, that's the main thing. Keep your own interests going as much as possible to keep your individuality. Don't follow the crowd – do what's right for you. Don't expect everything to be perfect – keep your sense of humour. Don't be a bore about your pregnancy and babies. There are so many other interesting things to talk about."

"Always listen to your children. A lot of what they say is tedious, once they've mastered the art of talking, but how else can you get to know them as individuals, and learn if anything is bothering them? Sometimes important points come out in seemingly unimportant chatter.

Working at a relationship doesn't have to be a chore. It really just involves considering the other person's feelings all the time.

Whether children bring you closer or force you apart depends on how much your ideas on childrearing coincide."

"To talk and listen to each other. Sometimes it can be very hard to express a feeling if the other partner does not listen or doesn't want to listen in case they feel they are being told off or blamed."

"Always talk to each other. Be there for one another. Never forget that you *both* have needs, not just the children."

"That communication between you is vital … you need to take time out to find ways of making each other feel special."

"Read, learn more about relationships and family values. Also, most important, work hard to keep the channels of communication open."

The next, sad, contribution comes from a childless woman of 54:

"Lack of communication was the cause of my marriage breakdown, because I was not aware that my husband didn't want children. He never discussed it with me as such, and so I was naive enough to believe that we would eventually have them, regardless of his wishes. It took 14 years of marriage for me to understand otherwise. I was at fault too, because I didn't pursue the issue vigorously enough. I am now divorced and I feel cheated in life, empty and lonely because I will never have a family union."

"It's too easy over time to sit down of an evening in front of the TV and switch off from one another. Make an effort for each other! Couples shouldn't forget that they are a couple and not just a family. Sometimes it's easy to let things get stale. You have to work hard and allow time to be together on your own to talk, laugh, make love."

"Go out to dinner once a week or have dinner at home alone with wine, and discuss everything. If possible, give your partner a day off from the responsibilities of home, or give her one night a week out with her friends."

"Keep one evening a week for yourselves as soon as possible after the baby is born (with our last baby we took nearly seven months to achieve this), and on that evening, cook a special meal and have a bottle of wine, and just talk about yourselves and enjoy being together again."

"I think the key issue is knowing yourself. How can any relationship survive if you don't? You also need honesty, respect, and your own time and space. Learn to communicate freely and to listen. Learn to give and take, love and be loved."

"We don't have a television. Therefore as partners and as a family we converse together and do things together perhaps more than the average family. Mealtimes are also very important – eating together as a group.

Not abusing the trust we place in each other. We may well do this mentally, i.e. fantasizing 'I wish he were dead', or 'the prince will come', but in real life not taking any step that would break our trust.

Never putting each other down in front of anyone – slag him/her off in private – we all do it to each other (?) – but it's a betrayal to take it outside the safety of home.

Help each other. Share responsibility. You do the washing up – he puts the nappies in soak. I mow the grass, he empties the dishwasher. Keeping it as non-sexist/stereotyped as strength/commonsense will allow. Helping each other equals supporting the partnership.

Our partnership has required considerable negotiation over the years, which, coupled with compromise, has probably helped our marriage survive.

It is important not to take any relationship for granted. Retaining a small amount of uncertainty keeps you on your toes. You can't neglect (either physically or mentally) a relationship and then wonder why the other person sought comfort elsewhere.

It's good for our marriage to argue occasionally – to clear the air – but never to carry it on long enough to breed resentment and to *always* be able to say sorry and admit when you are wrong."

On putting your partner first

"Try to always put each other first. Try not to take all your problems out on each other. Talk over everything, but don't forget to *listen* to what your partner says and also to what he doesn't say. Learn to laugh together."

"One day your children move off into the world and all that is left is the relationship you have built. I always tried to put my husband first and it has worked: we have been married 30 years."

"Remember when your children are grown and gone you will need each other."

"Having children does shift the focus of your relationship, but I think it's important to remember that one day they will lead lives of their own and it will be back to just the two of you, so make sure you take time for each other as well – even the best relationship will break down without communication. Talk to and listen to each other."

"I think it's important to keep children in perspective in a marriage. My husband is the most important to me, closely followed by our children. The children know he comes first, and are now old enough to understand this. I want to keep the relationship I have with my husband, and if we don't work at it for ourselves now, while the children are here, there may be nothing left once the children leave home. I don't think this is likely to happen in our case, but I do know of friends who have found they've nothing left once the children have grown up, as all their energies have gone into the children's lives and they haven't considered themselves."

"I never allowed the baby to rule our lives: we always felt in charge. That is the golden rule, I think – the baby comes after your love and companionship and therefore should not overrule that relationship. I think I did this quite successfully for many years. It seems when 'baby' grows up and gets married and they are independent, they become more like siblings than offspring – which is why having my children was one of the best things I ever did and I never regretted giving birth five times.

I think mothers can easily lose their identity. This can start from the moment she is visited in hospital after the birth, when everyone seems to be bringing the baby something. Learn to take time out for yourself and don't be afraid to ask your partner for help."

"Be prepared to devote large chunks of your life to your children, but not at the expense of neglecting your partner, as when the children grow up, it's important you still have something to share together. We love our children but the boy was an absolute nightmare to bring up, and it put a great strain on our relationship. We solved our problems by seeking help when we realized we needed it, and by not being scared to admit that sometimes as parents we were 'failing'. Now they have left home, we don't want anything to rock the boat between us. Parenthood is about survival, caring, hanging on when times get tough, seeing the children's point of view and having time together as a couple – not always being with the children 24 hours a day."

"Make sure you still make time for each other. The children have my time from 7am to 7pm, and from 7pm to 7am is the parents' time. It is important not to forget that you have identities in your own right and aren't just mum and dad, so the children do not take over your whole life and drive a wedge between you.

We are very lucky because we are a very close couple. All the bad times that we have had in the past – my husband's nervous breakdown, my miscarriage, severe financial difficulties – have drawn us closer together. We give each other support and talk through our problems."

The next contribution is from a widower:

"When the brood is up and flown the nest, mothers don't feel as needed as they used to when the kids were young. All they seem to have to do is the housework and shopping – this makes them feel taken for granted. I used to leave little love notes in different places round the house. 'I love you' (stuck to the salt cellar); 'I want you' on top of the washing machine on a Saturday morning (I usually had Saturday off); 'I want to hold you' (stuck to the washing-up liquid); 'I want to kiss you' (under her pillow); 'You're my peaches and cream' (stuck to a tin of peaches); 'Hello Sexy' (below the mattress – she turned the mattress every week)."

And finally, remember that:

"Love sees you through virtually every one of life's obstacles."

CONCLUSION

The hundreds of people who took part in this survey have made their own contributions to the debate on marriage that currently rages in Britain.

It seems clear that marriage is becoming less popular, especially among women who are disillusioned by the lack of support they get from men in running the home and family. Because of this lack of support, the numbers of single mothers are rising dramatically. Whether we like it or not, society is changing, and young people growing up in this changing world need all the help they can get to take their part in it.

Marriage as an institution may be dying, but people will go on trying to make lasting relationships because of the potential for happiness they hold. Yet children who live in loveless homes and have no role models to learn from are surely going to find it more difficult to form satisfying partnerships themselves.

Our education system could provide children with an invaluable extra dimension of personal skills. One contributor points the way forward:

"Marriage and parenthood should be part of education in schools. Everyone needs a real awareness of what relationships are about. I don't think there would be so many broken homes if people were properly prepared and informed before they got married or set up home together."

The way we understand and get on with other people – not just our lovers or partners and our children but parents and friends, employers and colleagues, and even people we speak to in the street or on the phone and will never get to know – has a fundamental effect on the quality of our lives. Communication, understanding and cooperation enable individuals to live together and communities to flourish, yet the study of psychology, which investigates people's attitudes, beliefs and values, and offers creative ways of dealing with personal problems, is glaringly absent from the National Curriculum in schools.

Until recently, sex education was a compulsory subject for all schoolchildren, but now – at a time when the spread of AIDS makes it more necessary than ever – the government has removed it from the National Curriculum. It has also removed some of the more expensive brands of Pill from the list of freely available contraceptives, probably as a prelude to stopping free prescriptions for all contraceptives. These moves are likely to increase the number of unwanted teenage pregnancies.

The study of psychology and sex education is the background against which young people can form their own ideas about personal responsibility. Personal development skills are best learned through discussion and debate: listening to other people's points of view and feeling free to experiment with your opinions, to change and broaden your perspective, is what creates tolerance and understanding. The debate in this book is about the realities of living together in the 1990s. It's a debate that could help couples rethink and improve some aspects of their lives, a debate that could give people who have yet to try it a more realistic expectation of what it's like to share – or try to share – the responsibility of running a home and family.

If this debate became part of every adolescent's education, people could grow up to make more informed choices about living together, couples could make their own personal contracts about sharing responsibility, and relationships would undoubtedly have a better chance of surviving.

USEFUL ADDRESSES

GREAT BRITAIN

Alcohol Abuse

Alcoholics Anonymous
PO Box 1, Stonebow House, York
Tel. 0904 640026

Childbirth

Active Birth Centre
55 Dartmouth Park Road, London NW5 1SL
Tel. 071 267 3006
Active birth, water birth services

Caesarean Support Group
55 Cooil Drive, Douglas, Isle of Man
Tel. 0624 661269
Non-medical support caesarean birth

Miscarriage Association
c/o Clayton Hospital, Northgate, Wakefield WF1 3JS
Tel. 0924 200799
Information, support for women, families

National Childbirth Trust
Alexandra House, Oldham Terrace, London W3 6NH
Tel. 081 992 8637
Sae with enquiries

Childcare

Gingerbread
35 Wellington Street, London WC2E 7BN
Tel. 071 240 0953
Support for one-parent families

National Council for One Parent Families
255 Kentish Town Road, London NW5 2LX
Tel. 071 267 1361
Support for one-parent families

Working Mothers Association
77 Holloway Road, London N7 8JZ
Tel. 071 700 5771
Self-help organisation for working parents

Family Planning

Brook Advisory Centres
153a East Street, London SE17 2SD
Tel. 071 708 1234
Free advise on contraception, sexual and emotional matters for under 25s.

Family Planning Association
27-35 Mortimer Street, London W1N 7RJ
Tel. 071 636 7866

Marie Stopes Clinic
108 Whitfield Street, London W1P 6BE
Tel. 071 388 0662
Family planning, abortion, male/female sterilisation

Family Therapy

Institute of Family Therapy
43 New Cavendish Street, London W1M 7RG
Tel. 071 935 1651

Marriage Guidance

British Association of Sexual and Marital Therapists
Whiteley Wood Clinic, Wooffinden Road, Sheffield S10 3TL
Tel. 0742 309827

The London Marriage Guidance Council
76a New Cavendish Street, London W1
Tel. 071 580 1087

RELATE (formerly the Marriage Guidance Council)
Herbert Gray College, Little Church Street, Rugby CV21 3AP
Tel. 0788 573241

Mental Health

MIND (National Association for Mental Health)
22 Harley Street, London W1N 2ED
Tel. 071 637 0741

Pre-Menstrual Syndrome

National Association for Pre-Menstrual Syndrome
PO Box 72, Sevenoaks, Kent TA13 1XQ

The Pre-menstrual Society
Verona, Hare Hill, Addlestone, Weybridge, Surrey, KT15 1DT

Rape Crisis Centres

Rape and Sexual Abuse Support Centre
PO Box 908, London SE25 5EL
Tel. 081 688 0332
Free support, advice and counselling

Rape and Sexual Abuse Support Line
c/o Council for Volunteer Services,
St Thomas Centre, Langley Road, Watford, Herts WD1 3PN
Tel. 0923 241600
Support line, individual counselling

Domestic Violence

London Women's Aid
52-54 Featherstone Street, London EC14 8RT
Tel. 071 251 6537

Rescue
PO Box 855, London W4 4JF
Tel. 081 995 4430
Refuge from domestic violence, campaigning

The Everyman Centre
30a Brixton Road
London SW9 6BU
Tel. 071 793 0155
Helpline for men who batter women

HELPLINES FOR AUSTRALIA AND NEW ZEALAND

AUSTRALIA

Abortion and Contraception Advisory Service
116 Wellington Parade, East Melbourne, Victoria 3002
Tel. 03 419 1686

Childbirth and Education Association of Victoria
761 Burwood Highway, Ferntree Gully, Victoria 3165
Tel. 03 758 7813

Childhood and Parenting Association of Victoria
49 Taylors Road, Croydon, Victoria 3136
Tel. 03 725 4832

Family Planning Association of Queensland
100 Alfred Street, Fortitude Valley, Queensland 4006
Tel. 08 252 5151

Family Planning Association of Victoria
259 Church Street, Richmond, Victoria 3121
Tel. 03 429 1868

Mid-life and Menopause Support Group
Room 6, Agnes Walsh House,
KEMH, Bagot Road, Subiaco, Western Australia 6008
Tel. 09 380 4444

Pre-menstrual Support Group of Victoria
9 Quixley Grove, Wantirna, Victoria 3152
Tel. 03 801 2001

NEW ZEALAND

Child and Family Services
93 Harewood Road, Christchurch
Tel. 03 3523409

Family Therapy Centre
6 Goring Road, Sandringham
Tel. 09 8466306

Hutt Valley Alcohol and Drug Service
47 Dilmuir Street, Lower Hutt
Tel. 06 5694540

Mac Dunedin Men's Action on Domestic Violence
PO Box 5370, Dunedin
Tel. 03 4879246

Maori Men for Non Violence
Te Matauranga O Tane
St John's Street, Optki
Tel. 07 3155477

Marriage Guidance NZ
PO Box 1688, Dunedin
Tel. 03 4879246

Marriage Guidance
Corner Armagh and Montreal Streets, Christchurch
Tel. 03 3668804

National Collective of Rape Crisis and Related Groups of Atoearoa Inc.
PO Box 6181, Te Aro Wellington
Tel. 85667678

Women's Refuge
PO Box 16192, Sandringham
Tel. 09 3033939